THE
AUTISM JOB CLUB

THE
AUTISM JOB CLUB

The Neurodiverse Workforce in the
New Normal of Employment

MICHAEL S. BERNICK

RICHARD HOLDEN

Skyhorse Publishing

Dedication to:

Donna, once again
—msb

Ricardo, William, and Gaelen
—rjh

Skyhorse Publishing books may be purchased in bulk at special discounts
for sales promotion, corporate gifts, fund-raising, or educational purposes.
Special editions can also be created to specifications. For details, contact the
Special Sales Department, Skyhorse Publishing, 307 West 36th Street, 11th
Floor, New York, NY 10018 or info@skyhorsepublishing.com.

Skyhorse® and Skyhorse Publishing® are registered trademarks of Skyhorse
Publishing, Inc.®, a Delaware corporation.

Visit our website at www.skyhorsepublishing.com.

10 9 8 7 6 5 4 3 2 1

Library of Congress Cataloging-in-Publication Data is available on file.

Cover design by Georgia Morrissey
Cover photo credit: Shutterstock

ISBN: 978-1-63220-696-1
Ebook ISBN: 978-1-63220-997-9
Printed in the United States of America

CONTENTS

FIGURES

INTRODUCTION

Creating a Place in the Emerging Job World

This book is about building a better structure of employment for adults with autism.

It addresses how adults with autism and their families and advocates can best approach their own employment searches. More broadly, it addresses how collectively we can build a more effective autism employment system.

At the start, we should say that while we hope this book finds an audience in the autism community, we believe it also speaks to a wider community of workers. Our focus is on autism employment. But autism is a proxy for other neurodiverse workforces. Further, as we argue throughout the book, many of the employment challenges faced by adults with autism reflect the employment challenges most workers will face in our highly competitive and rapidly evolving job world.

Adults with autism are the fastest growing group among the neurodiverse workforces. Yet, the high numbers of persons on the disability rolls, the high unemployment and underemployment rates, and the difficulties of navigating and competing in the job world are characteristics of these other workforces, just as they are of the autism workforce. Additionally, the employment strategies for the autism workforce—the job search and networking techniques, identifying opportunities in the different industry sectors and occupations, the craft ethos and the retraining ethos—are equally relevant to these other neurodiverse workforces. Indeed, in these employment strategies lie greater effectiveness in navigating the job world for all workers.

Increasingly, the public policy questions linked to the high unemployment among the autism workforce also are policy questions applicable to the general population. How much more costly is it to find employment for adults with autism than to maintain these adults on government benefit rolls—as is largely being done today—and what are the benefits? How much can government operated or funded programs increase employment and what should these programs look like? What is the role of extra-governmental associations, and how can these associations best be structured?

***

The book draws on our experiences in recent years in the job placement of adults with autism, as well as research on other autism employment projects nationwide. It also draws on employment research we have undertaken over the past thirty-five years and our experiences with job placement during this time.

I (Michael Bernick) first entered the job training world in 1979, as a volunteer with a community job training agency, the San Francisco Renaissance Center, and later spent five years in the 1980s as director of Renaissance. In the late 1990s and early 2000s, I served as director of the California state labor department, the Employment Development Department, where I first became involved with placement programs for adults with autism. Since leaving EDD in 2004, I have continued this involvement.

Autism has exploded into public consciousness during the past decade, spawning hundreds of blogs, websites, articles, and books. Though most of these books focus on early education and intervention or K–12 education, increasingly books are appearing on autism employment. Written usually by vocational counselors or job coaches, these book usually do offer good advice on such job search strategies as identifying job openings, using job boards, getting in the door, networking. These are important topics and we address them in a section on job search skills and the role of the autism job coach.[1]

This book differs from others on autism employment in addressing further the most effective collective employment efforts, rooted in an understanding of the evolution of the job world in the United States and the opportunities being created. We examine autism employment relating to the technology sector, the rise of the Internet commerce and social media economy, and the resilience of the non-tech, practical economy. We also address two major job dynamics that go across sectors and occupations and their meaning for autism employment: the heightened competition for most jobs; and the breakdown of full-time employment and rise of project-based, contingent, and part-time employment.

Getting a job was a challenge when I started in job training in 1979. It is significantly more difficult today. Most adults with autism will seek full-time employment with a stable company, as they should; and fortunately there are many jobs still out there that fit this category. Further, there is a small but growing number of employers who affirmatively seek out workers with autism (often because of a family tie). But for adults with autism, as for all workers, the effort needed to land a job will be far greater than in previous decades. They and their support teams will need to utilize a number of the job search strategies and also strategies of on-going skills upgrading, retraining, and lifelong learning.

We may have reached a tipping point in achieving fuller employment for adults with autism, due to the coming together of the demographics of autism, the movement toward inclusion, and the out-of-control growth of government disability benefit programs. But it will take effort to translate these social forces into job placements. A part of this effort will be through government, specifically government-funded projects. A larger part will be through the extra-governmental autism community efforts that are prevalent today and have the capacity to expand.

***

This book arises from an essay that first appeared in *Zócalo Public Square*, which attracted considerable interest in our Autism Job Club.

In deciding to develop the essay into a book, I turned to Richard Holden, with whom I had worked at EDD (he was the EDD labor market research director) and who in 2004 became the regional commissioner of the Bureau of Labor Statistics (BLS). richard is one of the most knowledgeable labor market specialists in the United States. The book is written mainly in my voice, as someone involved with autism employment on a local and personal level. But its ideas and strategies are informed by Richard's research and experience. It has been a true partnership.

***

I joined the autism community in 1991, when my son William was diagnosed with autism. When he was younger, I wrote at times about his behaviors and struggles for inclusion. As he got into his teens, I stopped writing about him, mainly for privacy reasons.

His ongoing employment search is included in Chapter 5. Privacy reasons led me to omit certain details and experiences. However, I felt it was important to include at least a part of his story, since it is the one that I know best and since it also illustrates the challenge ahead for much of our autism community. The literature on autism employment often refers to main impediments like the lack of social skills or eye contact or challenges posed by the interview process. In most cases, the obstacles are more formidable than these impediments— even as they are conquerable.

Part I
The Six Autism Employment Strategies

At a number of points in this book, reference is made to "persons with disabilities." This is the term used by the Bureau of Labor Statistics in data collection and often by other researchers and practitioners. It includes adults with autism along with adults with other neurodiverse conditions and with physical conditions (hard of hearing, loss of sight, wheelchair use).

We emphasize from the outset that we use this term reluctantly. It is a term that emphasizes limitations, rather than strengths, and that invites inappropriate condescension and pity. Most of all, it is a term without true meaning. All workers have limitations and strengths in work tasks; all of us perform different tasks with different levels of competence.

Within the autism and neurodiverse community, the use of other more accurate terms is spreading, and employment groups are arising with names such as Expandability and Positive Resource Center. Our hope is that the phrase "workers with disabilities" will go the way of other previous terms (i.e. "handicapped," "challenged") that we now regard as outdated.

1

WE COME TOGETHER AS THE AUTISM JOB CLUB: INTRODUCING SIX AUTISM EMPLOYMENT STRATEGIES

The Laughing Vanguard

ON THE FIRST Saturday of each month, the Bay Area Autism Job Club gathers at the ARC building, located at 11th and Howard in San Francisco's South of Market area. Fifteen or so adults with autism are in attendance, ranging in age from early twenties to fifties, and even one member, James Ullrey, age seventy-two.

It is not easy to see the Autism Job Club as the vanguard of change for workers with autism. At the meetings, club members will laugh inappropriately or talk to themselves, go off topic, stare into space, wander around. Though many of the members have at least some college education—and a significant number have college degrees—they all are on the employment margins. Some are unemployed; most have part-time or contingent lower wage employment. The club meetings focus on relatively basic job search skills, résumé skills, and interviewing skills.

Yet, the Autism Job Club, and hundreds of other local groups across the United States, are experimenting with new employment projects and structures for workers with autism and other neurodiverse conditions—cerebral palsy, dyslexia, learning disabilities. It is an effort pushed forward by the unsustainable rise in costs of government disability programs, changing social views, and most of all, the fierce energy and extra-governmental efforts of families and friends of workers with neurodiverse conditions.

Autism: A True Spectrum

"If you've met one person with autism, you've met one person with autism," Temple Grandin responds when asked about the characteristics of persons with autism. Ms. Grandin, a professor of animal science and inventor who was diagnosed with autism as a child, has been a presence in the autism community nationwide since the early 1980s, with separate memoirs published in 1986 *(Emergence: Labeled Autistic)* and 1996 *(Thinking in Pictures)*. She became known to a wider population in 2010 through the movie, *Temple Grandin,* in which she was portrayed by actress Claire Danes.

Adults with autism span a wide range of skills, abilities, education levels, and interests. Much of the conventional wisdom regarding work skills and deficiencies of persons on the spectrum is wrong. Adults on the spectrum, for example, do not all excel in areas of math or science (most don't) or are "little geniuses." At the same time, adults on the spectrum are not all plagued by social isolation or difficulties/a lack of interest in workplace relations (many are very social).

So it is with the diversity of skills and abilities in our autism job club, as is clear from our first meetings. In early November 2011, the Autism Asperger Syndrome Coalition for Education Networking and Development (AASCEND), the volunteer group of adults with autism and their friends and families, posted a note to its members regarding the formation of a job club. At the first meeting, on Saturday, November 19, forty of us gathered in a small classroom at the City College campus in downtown San Francisco. As we went around the room, the participants described their job status and job searches, which varied widely. Here is how each participant described himself or herself at the time:

1. Paul, fifty-four, has a handyman business in Stockton that he has been trying to build up. He has a BA degree in geography from Fresno State and has held a few jobs in the field that didn't last long. This led him to self-employment.
2. Andrew, thirty-two, completed two years of college and is working part-time with a recycling company while pursuing his sculpturing and design work.
3. Alex, thirty-one, has a BA degree in child/adolescent education from San Francisco State University. His job history includes short-term stints as a courtesy clerk at a large supermarket, a busman at a coffee shop chain, and a four-month position in the technology department of a major hotel. He currently is volunteering at the ARC while he looks for a job.
4. Gabriel, twenty-eight, has some college credits and is doing short-term transcription gigs he finds through family contacts while he seeks a full-time job.
5. Mark, early forties, worked in the information technology field for fifteen years as a consultant. His business partner, who was responsible for business development, passed away four years ago, the company fell apart, and Mark has not worked steadily since.
6. Martha, late twenties, has a masters degree, but has been able only to find work twelve hours a week as a clerk in a small legal office. She seeks more steady work, perhaps in a job related to her library science degree.
7. Jim, seventy-two, is the senior member of the group. He has college degrees in physics and chemistry and worked for Apple on a project basis a few years back. Mainly, though, he has worked in non-technology jobs: delivering pizza, doing yard work, supervising an after-school program for youth. He is not working now, but at seventy-two, still in the market for work.

The Autism Job Club Comes Together and Branches Out

Since that first meeting in November 2011, a number of the original participants have stopped coming. Some have found jobs, others have drifted out. Meanwhile new members have joined the group. The club is a fluid one; members come for as long or short a time as they find value. Some participants are employed or in school but come to improve their job search skills for future employment.

We rely mainly on volunteers—counselors, parents, graduate students. Cindy Zoeller is a workforce career coach in Sacramento who heard about the job club and drove ninety miles to the organizational meeting. She volunteers as the club facilitator, preparing the agenda and handouts and leading each session. She is joined by John Comegys, a job coach from Dixon who comes to volunteer, along with four graduate students from San Francisco State University.

The meetings start with an update on our job searches and a sharing of job leads. Each meeting then focuses on a specific job-search technique: using job boards, interviewing, preparing a résumé, getting in the door through part-time or contingent work, resolving issues that arise on the job. In between meeting dates, Ms. Zoeller keeps in touch with individual members to discuss their specific job situations and job searches.

Beyond the job placement activities, the club soon branched out in 2012 and early 2013 with other employment strategies. Brian Jacobs, a venture capitalist and job club volunteer, launched a LinkedIn site, Spectrum Employment Community by AASCEND. The site is an online discussion board for job club members, as well as an online job board and an online reference for employers. It is also a reference for parents and advocates seeking to keep up with latest information on employment for workers with autism.

In 2012, two club members, Luby and Andy Aczel, started a combination business/training agency, The Specialists Guild (Guild). The Guild is aimed at training persons with autism for employment in software testing—an occupation which the Aczels believe can be uniquely suited to persons with autism. The Aczels and other club members also built an autism technology employment network to promote hiring with Bay Area technology firms.

Laura Shumaker started a popular autism blog for the *San Francisco Chronicle*. She volunteered to research and report on autism employment efforts elsewhere in California.

The Six Strategies for Autism Employment

In this book, we draw on the experiences of our club members and club activities. We also draw on the experiences of other autism employment projects throughout the United States. The field is a very active one, with adults with autism, parents, and advocates coming together and new projects being launched regularly.

The following chapters are structured around two main lines of argument arising from these experiences. The first is that an improved autism employment system will be a series of strategies. Just as there is no "right" industry sector or occupation for all adults with autism, there is not a single strategy for our collective employment efforts. The technology sector will offer employment opportunities for adults with autism. So too will the Internet economy—some jobs directly in Internet economy firms, more jobs in the Internet economic activity of the share economy and social mission economy. The greatest number of jobs will be in the practical economy, of health aides, retail clerks, bakers, and repair persons. Job placement will involve multiple sectors as well as strategies of autism job coaches, on-going skills gains, supported work, and workplace culture.

We also explore the roles and limits of government programs. Government programs for adults with autism have continued to expand over the past twenty-five years since the passage of the Americans with Disabilities Act. Yet, the unemployment rate of adults with autism has not significantly declined. Why is this so, since, while placement performance is uneven among programs, most of the programs do place participants into jobs? Even if doubled in size, though, the programs would only reach a small part of the population. Government programs alone can never be the answer. A broad employment network outside of government is needed. Such a network is slowly emerging and its expansion has to be a priority.

In the first section of this book (Chapters 2–6), we discuss the Autism Job Club and the adult autism community in the United States today and its employment status. We start in the next chapter by saying more about the ways that club members have come together to protect each other as well as to seek collective approaches to housing, social networks, and employment futures.

In Chapter 3 we turn to the explosion in autism numbers in the United States and autism presence in public consciousness. Three decades ago, autism was a condition little known and little covered. Today it is difficult to pick up a newspaper or magazine or turn on the television without seeing a reference to autism.

Despite this sea change in autism's role in American society, the employment of workers has not changed much in the past three decades and more, as set out in chapter 4. An estimated 60 to 70 percent of persons with autism are unemployed. Many sustain themselves financially through government benefit rolls, especially through the Supplemental Security Income (SSI) and Social Security Disability Insurance (SSDI) programs—the latter which has skyrocketed in numbers in the past few decades. In Chapter 5, we examine the background and employment journey of one adult with autism, illustrating in some detail the employment obstacles. In Chapter 6, we examine the backgrounds and employment journeys of several other club members, illustrating the variety of employment histories.

In the second section of the book (Chapters 7–19), we build on the first section and on our examination of autism employment initiatives which have been undertaken in recent years. Our findings lead us to six strategies that, taken together, can begin to reshape the nature of employment for adults with autism. These strategies are: (i) the art of the autism job coach, (ii) autism and technology advantage,

(iii) autism and the emerging Internet economy, (iv) autism and the practical/craft economy, (v) autism and supported employment, and (vi) autism, lifelong learning, and workplace culture.

Our Collective Journey

As we shall see in the pages ahead, the employment journeys of our job-club members, especially those of the older members, have been difficult ones. For them, getting a job rarely leads to employment stability. Our members may be slower than others to pick up tasks, behave in inappropriate manners, not appear on time, or lose jobs in the largely unforgiving job world.

Some job placement projects for adults with autism focus today on interviewing skills and improving eye contact, and making a positive presentation. All of these are valuable skills and our Autism Job Club seeks to teach them. Cindy Zoeller has sessions to videotape mock interviews and review them with our members.

Yet, the obstacles facing our members usually go way beyond eye contract. These obstacles may involve major cognitive gaps and information processing gaps. They may involve major gaps in judgment. They may involve a lack of executive skills—including knowing what to do and being able to act effectively if a job is lost.[2]

The building of a better employment system for adults with autism will take the active efforts of all of us. It will involve pilot projects, experiments, and missteps. It will mean building on thousands of different efforts across the United States by adults with autism, parents, and advocates coming together.

The FRED conference in Los Angeles for "special needs adults" is one of the main annual national conferences involving the autism community. In March 2014, the panel on employment was the featured panel, and the conference lead, Ms. Mari-Anne Kehler, opened by stating, "Nothing says purpose and living with meaning like employment." Then followed several references by the panel moderator, an attorney in the San Gabriel Valley, to the "incredible" skills of our young adults with disabilities and the "amazing" employment projects they were involved in, that were paving the way to fuller employment.

The employment opportunities that the participants described, though, were very modest: a job at a small restaurant in Albuquerque; a micro-business in animation started by a college student with autism in Southern California; a series of small ventures in laundry service, premium candles, and office services by a non-profit autism agency in Chapel Hill. Looked at one way, the number of jobs generated was miniscule; the claims of fuller employment exaggerated.

Yet looked at another way, something unusual and noteworthy was going on in the conference room. The presenters and audience were not whining or complaining or presenting themselves as victims. Nor were they waiting for government to do something. Against all odds, they were trying to generate employment for themselves and others, to engage in mutual support, to work *with* government, but also outside of government.

The autism community's efforts toward a better employment system are still in their very early stages. We are in a wilderness that we only partly understand, and on a road that is not clearly marked. We have much to discover.

Come join our collective journey in the next chapters as we examine who we are, what we have learned so far, and strategies for advancing on this journey.

2

THE AUTISM JOB CLUB AS
VOLUNTARY ASSOCIATION
AND MUTUAL SUPPORT

THE EXTRA-GOVERNMENTAL NETWORK—THE voluntary association of adults with autism, parents, and advocates—is at the center of autism employment efforts.

It will be valuable at this starting point to say a little about one such network, the Autism Asperger Syndrome Coalition for Education Networking and Development (AASCEND) of the Bay Area. It was AASCEND that created our Autism Job Club in 2011 and that oversees its activities.

AASCEND is entirely outside of government. It receives no government funds and depends on volunteer time, effort, and resources. Each of us, those "on the autistic spectrum" and the "neurotypicals," has taken a different path to AASCEND. Most of us have found in AASCEND a community we had sought for some time.

AASCEND started in 1999 as a support group for the adult autism community of the Bay Area. But it has developed over the years into far more. It is a network in which members act to "cover the back" of other members. We get involved to help out if one of our members is taken advantage of or unfairly treated or facing homelessness or in need of assistance with legal issues (one of our members was charged last year with attempted murder). We rush to respond when we hear the firebell in the night from our community.

Further, AASCEND serves as a means of collective action to channel our fears, concerns, and hopes for ourselves, our children, and the broader adult autism community. Among the projects our members are interested in: a 577-acre new neighborhood in Sacramento with a focus on housing for adults with autism, an autism housing cooperative in Half Moon Bay, an autism social network and recreational group ("Friends Like Me"), and several employment structures, including an online autism employment network tied to LinkedIn.

***

I heard about AASCEND in summer 2011. I am not a joiner. Some years ago I served as a local elected official in the Bay Area, a member of the Bay Area Rapid Transit (BART) Board, and went to political events. But since leaving office in 1996 I have withdrawn from politics and its socializing. I rarely join in any political or social gatherings.

However, as my son William was entering adulthood, I wanted him (and me) to connect to the adult autism world. In September 2011, William and I attended an AASCEND meeting in a small classroom at the downtown campus of San Francisco City College, at Fourth and Mission.

There was nothing unusual about the meeting, attended by fifteen or so others. I can't even recall the subjects discussed. Yet I do remember thinking as the meeting ended, "I'm finally home."

***

AASCEND was founded in 1999 by a handful of adults on the autistic spectrum and family members, including Camilla and Ron Bixler.

The Bixlers had been involved in the autism community since the mid-1990s. Their son Andrew, born in 1981, was diagnosed as being on the autistic spectrum in 1994, at age fourteen. For years they had known that something was not quite right, that he did not interact with other children or teachers, that he spoke in sentences from videos he watched, that he struggled with subjects in school despite a good deal of assistance and tutoring.

With a handful of other parents, they set up the Star Academy, a private school in Marin for youth with autism and other neurodiverse conditions. The parents converted a church building that was in a state of disrepair into a school for thirty-five students. The parents themselves did the painting, recarpeting, and carpentry work.

In 1999, Camilla attended an autism conference at San Francisco State University. On one panel were three men in their forties identified as on the autistic spectrum: Paul Nussbaum, Greg Yates, and Adam Pollack. In the audience were others from the adult autism community including a man who kept tapping his left arm, Jim Ullrey, and Dave Van Etten, a friendly middle-aged father with a son on the spectrum. Camilla recalls: "We spoke after the presentation and thought, 'why not keep this going?' We set up bylaws and incorporated as AASCEND and began monthly meetings on subjects that we thought would be of interest to persons in the autism community. Health and dating were popular subjects in the first years, and they continue to be so today."

Throughout the next twelve years, the active membership in AASCEND ebbed and flowed but the Bixlers continued to be involved along with others from the first gathering (Paul, Greg, Adam, Jim, and Dave). Most AASCEND participants are adults with autism or relatives, but not all. Jack Fagan, for example, is an autism community advocate and autism self-help proponent. He was on the staff of the Supported Workshop at ARC and currently is an administrator at the Hamilton Family Center and has been active in AASCEND for over a decade.

In mid-2014, AASCEND had a contact list of 350 persons, built up over the years of those who have attended a meeting or expressed interest. Our monthly meetings range from twenty to forty persons, depending on the topic. Usually the attendees are divided roughly between an equal number of adults with autism and parents/advocates. Our board of directors has a minimum of 50 percent adults with autism.

There is no formal membership or membership fees. Anyone is welcome. We do not ask for any formal diagnosis. If someone considers himself or herself a member of the autism community, that is enough.

***

At the core of AASCEND are our members who regard their autism community involvement as a mission. First among these is Camilla Bixler.

Camilla taught in the San Francisco Community College District for over three decades before retiring in 2013. Now she spends most of her time on autism community volunteer efforts.

On a recent day, Camilla called around to find housing for Hank, one of our members in his forties whose life has been in a downward spiral the past few years. Hank has been living in a rented room in a house, but the owner is now selling. Hank's only source of income is SSI; he is on his own, with no family network. Camilla called the local nonprofits to try and find another room rental.

A few months earlier, Camilla was part of a team of AASCEND members who came to the aid of a member, Sloan, who had been fleeced in the sale of a vehicle. Sloan, in his early twenties, works as a bagger at Trader Joe's. At his job, he ran into a former classmate from Lincoln High School and agreed to purchase a car from this classmate for $1,200. Before he informed his father, Sloan went to the bank and withdrew all of the money from his account. The car was virtually worthless; it was not safe to drive and besides Sloan did not have a license. Sloan's father, Steve, contacted the classmate and his father and asked that Sloan's money be returned. They refused.

At that point, the AASCEND network sprang into action. An attorney volunteered to help draft a letter to the classmate requesting the return of the money on the grounds of fraud. When that did not succeed, the attorney helped the father draft a small-claims court complaint. Camilla volunteered to attend the small-claims court hearing along with Sloan and his father. At the hearing she spoke about adults with autism and the history of persons preying on the lack of sophistication and guileless nature of many of these adults. The small-claims court ordered full repayment of the $1,200.

Around the same time, Camilla received a call that Jim, one of AASCEND's original members and now in his seventies, had been arrested for attempted murder. Jim had become angry with a guest staying at his house and shot at him. The guest was not injured but Jim was arrested.

Camilla led a campaign of AASCEND members writing letters to the district attorney. Jim was placed on probation, with an ankle bracelet, and was able to avoid jail.

***

Beyond our extra-governmental social welfare network, AASCEND members are experimenting with broader structures to address housing, social isolation, and most of all, employment.

Dr. Lou Vismara is a member of our group who lives in Sacramento. Dr. Lou was a prominent cardiologist in California and is a graduate of Stanford and Baylor College of Medicine. He retired from his cardiology practice after his son Mark was diagnosed with autism. Since 2000, he has worked full-time on autism issues with the Office of the President Pro Tem of the California Senate.

One of his projects was the creation of the MIND Institute at UC Davis.[3] Another has been the development of an autism-focused community on 577 acres in the Natomas region of Sacramento. Dr. Lou began discussions in 2007 with a landowner of hundreds of acres in Natomas with ties to the autism community.

In a *Sacramento Bee* op-ed in 2009, he set out a vision for this community,[4] "where our children with autism, as well as other individuals with other disabilities and special needs, can thrive and optimize their potential across the lifespan." In a section worth quoting at length, he described the community.

> Because we're starting from scratch, we can create a true community that sustains the environment and supports all of its members. People of all background ages and abilities will live in a mix of some 3000 "green" single family homes, condos and apartments. A full 20 percent of the housing will be available to people with special needs, autism and other disabilities. A portion will also be set aside for seniors. The walkable community features shopping, jobs, parks and other recreation opportunities. A light rail station and an elementary school are slated to be built too.

> About 90 percent of autistic adults are unemployed . . . The employment opportunities we're working to establish for these most vulnerable citizens includes jobs on area farms and community gardens that will deliver locally grown fresh produce to the community.

> Living in close connection with the diverse group of people who will be drawn to this community will lend immeasurable richness to residents' lives, allowing them to tap deeply into their own humanity. It's the life many of us say we want. And it's the life I envision for Mark now and after I'm no longer able to care for him.

The Great Recession that began in 2009 halted development plans throughout Sacramento, including Dr. Lou's community. Today, five years later, development is only beginning to resume in Sacramento, and Dr. Lou is resuming the pursuit of his vision.

On a more modest scale, AASCEND members are closely following autism co-op housing experiments in Half Moon Bay and Sonoma in order to ensure safe housing for their children into the future. The

Sonoma project, Sweetwater Spectrum, is an operating $10.4 million residential community for sixteen adults with autism.[5] The "Big Wave" is a residential community linked to a farming enterprise in the planning stages on fourteen acres in Half Moon Bay for persons with autism and other neurodiverse conditions.

Pamela Buttery is an AASCEND member who was for many years a real estate partner with Lew Wolfe, the owner of the Oakland A's baseball team. For her, reducing the social isolation of autism has been a priority. In 2012, she contributed one million dollars to establish "Friends Like Me," with the goal of building a social network of activities and connections among adults with autism in the Bay Area. She joins the group on weekends on outings to A's games, Angel Island, and the American Conservatory Theatre.

***

Housing, social connections, community-building are all among the missions of our AASCEND members operating through their own structures, outside of government. But no issue begins to even approach the concern for, worry about, and efforts relating to employment.

AASCEND's current employment projects include the Autism Job Club and related to it, The Specialists Guild (software quality control training), the Spectrum Employment Network, and the technology employment network for hiring in the local technology firms. Among our most involved employment activists is the prominent Silicon Valley venture capitalist, Brian Jacobs.

Brian has been in Valley venture investment since 1988. He graduated with a degree in mechanical engineering from MIT and later earned a MBA from Stanford Business School. He started his current firm, Emergence Capital, in 2003, focusing on early stage software companies. By 2014, it has $600 million under management and has funded and helped build more than fifty software firms.

Brian was drawn to AASCEND as his son Clay was graduating from high school and entering college. "I began thinking of how to get involved with adult autism," he recalls.

I did Internet searches, but did not find a lot about adult autism. There is a lot about youth autism but much less about adults.

Clay was born in 1994. His diagnosis is a dual one: Asperger's syndrome and slow processing speed. He did graduate from high school and is a sophomore at Cal Poly San Luis Obispo. He is doing fine academically, and is on course to graduate. But like most parents, Allison and I look to the future, and are concerned about what lies in store for him and other persons with autism.

Allison attended an AASCEND conference in 2011 that she saw on the Internet and told me about it. I attended my first AASCEND meeting in 2012. Like others, I found a community that welcomed everyone, neurotypical as well as persons on the spectrum.

I have focused on employment since joining AASCEND. For Clay, this is probably less of a challenge than social participation, but it is an area I thought I could be most help with. My first project has been Spectrum Employment Network by AASCEND meant as an online employment network tied to LinkedIn. It is an attempt to harness the power of social networking for autism employment.

Social networking, whether it be Twitter, Facebook, LinkedIn, or the hundreds of other social media outlets, has taken over business and personal marketing in just the past few years. When we evaluate early stage businesses at Emergence Capital we look for a social network element. A business, in tech or in any other sector, cannot function without a social media strategy.

At Spectrum, we are trying to harness social networking for job placements. Spectrum hopefully will provide a forum for our members to interact, to learn about job openings, to post articles of interest on autism employment strategies, to educate employers, and to convince employers to list jobs.

Of course there is the conundrum we face: just as the market is dramatically increasing the value of social network skills, these are precisely the skills that many in our autism community lack. Most of our members are not savvy in attracting LinkedIn followers or utilizing the current LinkedIn to find open jobs or go much beyond posting a résumé. But that's what we're trying to figure out, since we cannot ignore the market direction.

***

The extensive extra-governmental efforts going on at AASCEND are being replicated in communities throughout the nation. Our challenges, particularly our employment challenges, are the same challenges faced by adults with autism and their families and advocates outside the Bay Area. In the next section, we say more about the adult autism communities and employment/unemployment throughout the nation, as well as the employment searches of some of our members.

Part II
The Adult Autism Community in the United States Today and Its Employment Status

3

THE AUTISM EXPLOSION IN NUMBERS AND IN PUBLIC CONSCIOUSNESS

THE PAST THREE decades have seen an explosion in autism numbers and an equal explosion in autism's place in the public consciousness. This period also has seen within the autism community a growing rejection of the view of autism as a disease to be cured or treated and advancement of values that persons with autism bring to the society and economy.

Growth in Numbers of Persons with Autism

Two million persons in the United States in 2013, including 730,000 persons aged under twenty-one, are estimated to have some form of Autistic Spectrum Disorders (ASD), ranging from severe autism to the "higher functioning" Asperger's syndrome. The numbers have gone up dramatically in the past few decades, particularly in the number of children diagnosed with ASD.[7]

In 2014, the Centers for Disease Control and Prevention (CDC) estimated that 1 in 68 children born in the United States is diagnosed with ASD. This is an increase in ASD diagnoses of nearly 80 percent in just the past decade and a ten-fold increase in diagnoses over the past forty years.[8] Among boys, the CDC estimates that the number

19

diagnosed with autism is 1 in 42—roughly 4.5 times more common among boys than girls (1 in 189).

"Why this increase?" is a most frequent question both within and outside the autism community. Improved awareness and diagnosis is one factor but it is by no means the only one. Mark Roithmayr, former president of Autism Speaks, a leading autism advocacy organization, gave the following explanation for the growth in numbers: "Better diagnosis, broader diagnosis, better awareness, and roughly 50 percent of 'we don't know.'"[9] In a similar vein, CDC Director Thomas Frieden has stated: "Doctors are getting better at diagnosing autism; communities are getting much better at providing services to children with autism, and CDC scientists are getting much better at tracking which kids in the communities we're studying have autism."[10]

Among our job club members born prior to 1980, nearly all went undiagnosed until the mid-1990s or later. Until the past two to three decades, our older job club members and other persons with forms of autism were considered strange, odd, or badly-behaved. But their behavior was not linked to a neurological condition. Greg, Paul, and Adam were well into their forties before they received a diagnosis of autism in the 1990s.

Beyond increased awareness, the rise of autism numbers is increasingly linked to a combination of genetic predisposition and environmental factors. Autism Speaks answers "What causes autism?" with a discussion of the genetic markers identified as linked to autism, and adds "In the presence of a genetic predisposition to autism, a number of non-genetic, or environmental, factors influence further a child's risk." Several genes have been identified as causing autism, accounting for around 15 percent of cases, and more than 100 genes or gene changes have been identified that increase the risk that a child will develop autism. "In most cases, genetics alone can't distinguish why one person has autism and another does not. Gene-environment interactions appear to be at play."[11] The National Institute of Child Health and Human Development (NICHHD) offers a similar explanation of genetics and environmental factors in autism causation—though it recognizes the inability of researchers at this time to pinpoint these environmental factors or the nature of causation. "A great deal of evidence supports the idea that genes are one of the main causes of ASD," the Institute explains. "If someone is susceptible to ASD because of genetic mutations, then certain situations might cause autism in that person. For instance an infection or contact with chemicals in the environment could cause autism in someone who is susceptible because of genetic mutations."[12]

The Autism Society, one of the oldest autism advocacy organizations in the world, approaches the question of causation by noting that "there is no known single cause for autism, but it is generally accepted that it is caused by abnormalities in brain structure or function. Brain scans show differences in the shape and structure of the brain in children with autism versus in neurotypical children." The Society, like NICHHD and Autism Speaks, points to "genetic vulnerability" and environmental factors. While no one gene has been identified as causing autism, it is likely that some children with "irregular segments of genetic code" are born with a susceptibility to autism. This susceptibility might be triggered by environmental toxins, more prevalent in the environment than in the past.[13]

Research on the genetics and environmental factors related to autism is ongoing and likely soon will yield greater insight on causation. The research, though, has not slowed down the increase in numbers, and is unlikely to do so in the near future.

Growth in Autism's Role in Public Consciousness

Beyond the growing autism numbers in recent years is the growing awareness of autism among the general public. As late as the early 1990s, few people knew about autism. To the extent there was awareness, it was mainly tied to the 1988 movie, *Rain Man*. Dustin Hoffman portrayed an autistic savant who had incredible powers of memory but was unable to live independently or find employment (modeled after the real-life autistic savant Kim Peek).

The sharp increase in the numbers of ASD diagnoses beginning in the 1990s dramatically heightened autism's profile. A small stream quickly became a river of newspaper articles, memoirs of parents and grandparents, novels, television shows, and movies. Awareness was enhanced whenever someone well-known made public the fact they had a family member with autism.

Sue Miller's novel *Family Pictures*, published in 1989, was about a severely autistic boy, Randall, and the impact of his autism on the family dynamics. Autism was so little understood at the time that the book jacket read "*Family Pictures* . . . spans forty years in the life of a large family that is deeply bonded by the stranger in their midst—an autistic child." The book stood out as the autistic character, Randall, was so unusual at the time.

By the first decade of the 2000s, storylines involving autistic characters had become so prevalent that they had given rise to a new genre of "autistic lit" or "aut lit." In *The Curious Incident of the Dog in the Night-Time* (2004), non-autistic English novelist Mark Haddon wrote from the point of view of an Asperger's teen. The book became an international best seller and was soon followed by other aut-lit novels, *Tilt* (Elizabeth Burns, 2004), *A Wild Ride up the Cupboards* (Ann Bauer, 2005), and *Eye Contact* (Cammie McGovern, 2007). In her 2010 novel, *House Rules*, mainstream mystery writer Jody Picoult featured an eighteen-year-old with Asperger's syndrome. Similarly, autistic characters have been prominently featured in the movies *Adam* (young man with Asperger's and his romance with a female neighbor), *Mercury Rising* (Bruce Willis must protect an autistic boy with savant skills), *Mozart and The Whale (*romance grows between a young man and young woman, both with autism) and, by far the finest autism movie to date, *Temple Grandin* (woman on autistic spectrum finds her place as professor of animal science/inventor).

Beyond the novels and movies have been dozens of memoirs by parents, siblings, grandparents, and people with autism. They have been augmented by hundreds of websites by parents and professionals chronicling their lives and the lives of people they know with autism. In 2014, it is almost impossible to click on an online newspaper or magazine, turn on the television, or go to a movie, without encountering some reference to autism.

Rejection of Autism as a Disease to be Cured

A further shift in the autism world in recent years involves the rejection of autism as a disease to be cured. This shift is sometimes known as the autism-rights movement or neurodiversity movement, and our job-club members have been active in this effort.

The shift has its roots in the Autism Network International writings by three people on the autism spectrum: Jim Sinclair, Donna Williams, and Kathy Grant. In the early 1990s, writing in their newsletter *Our Voice*, they challenged the conventional view of autism as a disease. They asserted that they didn't want to be "cured," and emphasized instead the beneficial perspectives that persons with autism could bring to the society and economy.

The growth of the Internet in the early 2000s fueled the movement, giving rise to online discussion groups and to multiple local and national autism advocacy organizations. To take one example, Ari Ne'eman was an undergraduate at the University of Maryland, Baltimore County, when he started the Autistic Self-Advocacy Network (ASAN) in 2006. Ne'eman and ASAN gained national attention in 2008 when they protested a campaign by the New York University Child Study Center to highlight the alleged devastation caused by the rise in cases of autism. The campaign was in the form of ransom notes, such as "We have your son. We will make sure he will no longer be able to care for himself or interact socially as long as he lives. This is only the beginning," that were each signed "Autism." The center had assumed that the campaign would win it praise and financial support. Instead, ASAN letters and social media complaints led to the ads being pulled.

Ne'eman has gone on to serve on state and federal commissions on autism and to tour the country meeting with local groups. He met with our job club members in 2012. In this meeting, he set out his critique of the autism establishment, especially Autism Speaks, for casting autism in a highly negative light and emphasizing cures over inclusion. He also set out his message of autism self-advocacy and inclusion in employment and education.

Our job club members, Greg, Paul, and Jim, have remained in contact with ASAN and active in autism identity activism. They appeared in a documentary film by filmmaker William Davenport, *Too Sane for this World* (2011), on the unusual skills of people with autism. They also appeared in *Citizen Autistic* (2013), Davenport's film challenging the money spent on cures for autism rather than facilitating inclusion.

A signature moment in the autism-identity movement occurred in late 2013 with what initially appeared to be a non-controversial op-ed by Suzanne Wright, a cofounder of Autism Speaks. Ms. Wright had founded Autism Speaks with her husband, Bob Wright, the former chief executive officer of the NBC network. Their activism was sparked by the autism of their grandson.

Ms. Wright's op-ed, posted on the organization's website on November 11, 2013, and entitled "Autism Speaks to Washington—A Call for Action," was framed around the autism "crisis." The first short paragraphs read as follows:

> This week is the week America will fully wake up to the autism crisis.
>
> If three million children in America one day went missing—what would we as a country do?
>
> If three million children in America one morning fell gravely ill— what would we as a country do?
>
> We would call out the Army, Navy, Air Force and Marines. We'd call up every member of the National Guard. We'd use every piece of equipment ever made. We'd leave no stone unturned.

Yet, we've for the most part lost touch with three million American children, and as a nation we've done nothing.

The op-ed went on to call for a national plan to address health care, housing, and education for the three million children with autism who cannot dress on their own or eat independently or care for themselves in any way.

Autism Speaks and Suzanne Wright expected the autism community to rally around the op-ed. Instead, the piece became a lightning rod for criticism of Autism Speaks and its depiction of the despair connected with autism. One of our members, Laura Shumaker, who writes the autism blog for the *San Francisco Chronicle* and is the mother of a twenty-seven year old with autism, wrote in the *Chronicle*, "I am feeling very discouraged by the recent remarks by Suzanne Wright." Schumaker went on to describe her previous participation in Autism Speaks and defense of the organization and how she felt betrayed by the op-ed. She then added a poignant description of her son, Matthew.

> My son Matthew was a very challenging kid to raise, and at times I felt hopeless and depressed. But he is now a delightful, earnest, quirky and loving 27 year old. We were recently at the San Francisco airport and before we boarded, he told the agent at the gate that he needed an early board pass (something I usually do for him). "Let me handle this," he told me assertively, and turned to the agent. "I have autism, and planes are hard."
>
> I tell Matthew every day, (sometimes twice a day), how proud I am of him, and how much I love him. He had a reputation for being aggressive and even violent, but he has grown and matured, and is a sweet gentle soul. He is currently attempting to get in touch with everyone who knew "the old Matthew" and tell them he is sorry. I admire him so much.

Laura Shumaker subsequently resigned her association with Autism Speaks.

John Elder Robison, a person with autism and the author of several popular books on autism,[14] also publicly resigned his association with Autism Speaks. Robison's lengthy blog posting on his resignation mixed recognition of the needs in the autism community with criticism of Autism Speaks for its focus on "cures" rather than services.

> I celebrate the gifts autism brings us, and I have discussed at length the emerging realization that autism—as a neurological difference—confers both gift and disability on everyone it touches. It's the fire that moves humanity forward, while simultaneously being a fire that can burn us individuals as we try to make our way.
>
> Mrs. Wright's op-ed articulates a view of the "autism situation" that is very different from my own. She says things I would never say to people with autism and cannot in good conscience stand by. . . . I have tried to help Autism Speaks staffers understand how destructive its messages have been to the psyches of autistic people. We do not like hearing that we are part of an epidemic. We are not problems for our parents or society, or genes to be eliminated. We are people.
>
> We do have problems, and we need help. Some of us need counseling or training, while others have significant medical challenges. We also need acceptance, and support. There is great diversity in our community, which means we have a very broad range of needs. Unfortunately, the majority of the research Autism Speaks has funded to date does not meet those needs, and the community services are too small a percentage of total budget to be truly meaningful.

The autism community is not monolithic; views differ widely on using the language of disease or cure. However, it is an indication of how far the autism community has changed in the past decade that references to the "plague" of autism are challenged, and that this challenge is coming from the community itself.

***

Given the sharply increased autism numbers, attention, and identity, increased employment rates might be expected to follow. But this has not occurred. Employment and unemployment rates for adults with autism have changed little in the past two decades, as we shall examine in the next chapter.

AUTISM EMPLOYMENT AND UNEMPLOYMENT TODAY

MOST OF OUR job club members are active in the labor market and are employed at least part-time or intermittently—though a full-time job with expectation of steady employment is the exception.

When considering all persons with autism, the employment situation is not as promising. The most widely used estimate of unemployment rate among persons with autism, though very rough, is in the range of 60 to 70 percent. Government disability rolls have skyrocketed in size in the past decade, with a good number of adults with autism going on these rolls in their twenties and not exiting.

As a result, a network of government and government-funded agencies and nonprofits has developed in order to help people with autism find employment. This network, though, mainly serves a small part of the autism workforce and places individuals in low-level, contingent positions.

Estimated Unemployment Rates for Persons with Autism

There is no direct measurement of employment and unemployment rates among persons with autism by the federal government or other governmental entities. What does exist at this time are a small number of independent studies—estimates based on interviews with persons with autism and job counselors—as well as government data on unemployment among a broader group of "workers with disabilities."

Among the leading independent studies of persons with autism and employment is a 2012 study by researchers at Washington University in St. Louis, led by Professor Paul Shattuck. The researchers used data from the National Longitudinal Transition Study, a ten-year study of youths who receive special education services. Young people with autism fall within this group, along with youth who have been classified with "mental disabilities," learning disabilities, and speech and language problems. The researchers tracked the youths for a six-year period as they left high school and moved into other pursuits. They tracked approximately 2,000 individuals, including 500 with autism.

The study, published in the journal *Pediatrics* in May 2012,[15] indicated that youths with autism had lower employment and post-secondary schooling rates than the other groups. Among the autistic youth, nearly 44 percent had attended some post-secondary institution (vocational education or two to four year college) during the first six years after high school. However, only 55 percent had held any paid employment during these six years. Most striking, nearly 35 percent had neither any educational participation nor employment over the full six years.[16]

This rate of 35 percent with no education or work participation was significantly higher than the comparable rates of neither post-secondary education nor employment of other youth served in special education: 26 percent of youth with mental disabilities, 7 percent of youth with speech and language problems, and 3 percent youth with learning disabilities.

An Associated Press report covering the study profiled one young person with autism who was twenty-one at the time and scheduled to graduate from high school but unlikely to attend college. "He wants a job but has found only unpaid internships and is currently working part-time and unpaid as a worker at a fastener factory," the report noted. Reflecting the views of many parents of youths with autism, his mother tells the reporter, "I'm very afraid" about his prospects for ever finding steady employment, "It keeps me up at night."[17] Professor Shattuck, the lead researcher added, "Many families with children with autism describe turning eighteen as falling off a cliff because of lack of services."

Several research papers on autism and employment draw on a mix of interviews with persons with autism and broader data on workers with disabilities for their estimates. These estimates often place unemployment among adults with autism at conservatively over 60 percent. Writing in the *Journal of Vocational Rehabilitation*, Dawn Hendricks of Virginia Commonwealth University summarizes:

"Even for individuals who are considered to be higher functioning, employment results are appalling. Adults experience underemployment, switch jobs frequently, have difficulty adjusting to new job settings, make less money than their counterparts, and are much less likely to be employed than typically developing peers, individuals with less severe language disorders, or individuals with learning disabilities."[18]

For the most part, the estimates of unemployment of persons with autism rest on the government data on the broader category of "workers with disabilities." This category includes workers with a variety of neurological and physical conditions. The U.S. Bureau of Labor Statistics includes disabilities as one of the categories for collection as part of the Current Population Survey (CPS) of 60,000 households nationwide. Participants first are asked to self-identify a physical or mental disability and then are asked about employment status.[19]

Based on the CPS data, the Bureau of Labor Statistics estimated that in May 2012, 15.4 million persons in the sixteen to sixty-four age range, the prime employment range, had some work-related disability. Among this group, only 28.2 percent were employed. The majority of these persons were classified as "Not in the labor force," as they were not actively looking for employment.[20]

Added to the current low employment rate of workers with disabilities is the fact that this rate has not increased at all over the past nearly twenty-five years since the passage of the Americans with Disabilities Act in 1990. Cornell faculty Richard Burkhauser and Andrew Houtenville and Federal Reserve economist Mary Daly have tracked employment rates of workers with disabilities since 1980. Employment was slightly over 36 percent in 1980. It rose to near 40 percent by 1990, but since has declined, and went down even during the employment boom years of 1996-2000.[21]

In addressing the unemployment rate for adults with autism, the national autism advocacy groups—Autism Speaks, Autism NOW, and the Autism Society—mainly reference the "workers with disabilities" data. On their websites and in forums, they cite these data in claiming more than two-thirds of adults with autism to be without paid employment. Autism Speaks has gone further on its website stating that in its own interactions with the autism community, "Autism Speaks has found that nine out of ten [adults with autism] either are unemployed or underemployed, regardless of their IQ or education level."[22] Autism Speaks notes that a college education or college degree is no guarantee of employment for persons with autism.

The Sharp Rise in Government Disability Insurance Rolls

Over the past two decades, the decline in the employment rate of workers with disabilities has been accompanied by a sharp increase in workers who are not looking for work and are receiving Social Security Disability Insurance (SSDI). SSDI is the federal program that provides benefits to working-age adults who are determined to be unable to work. The program was established in 1956 to extend coverage of social security to include not only retirees (who had been covered since the 1930s) but also workers with physical injuries or other physical or mental conditions that make certain work impossible.

During its first two decades, SSDI was a relatively modest program. From the early 1990s through the first decade of the 2000s, though, SSDI exploded in size. From 1989 through 2009, the number of adults twenty-five to sixty-four years of age receiving SSDI doubled from 2.3 percent of all workers to 4.6 percent. By the middle of 2014, nearly 9 million adult workers in the United States were unemployed and on the SSDI rolls. This growth occurred even as the rate of disability among working-age adults remained stable and even as the number of physically dangerous jobs declined. It has been driven by a surge in enrollments among workers with neurological conditions classified as disabilities, including autism.

Figure 4-1 shows the sharp rise in the number of adults receiving SSDI between 1967 and 2014. This growth in claimants has been accompanied by a rise in average monthly payments for both male and female claimants, increasing faster than the Consumer Price Index, as shown in Figure 4-2. Figure 4-3 shows the accompanying costs of SSDI, reaching *$10 billion per month* by June 2014.

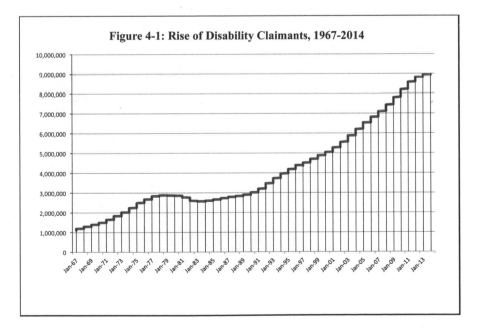

Figure 4-1: Rise of Disability Claimants, 1967-2014

Source: http://www.ssa.gov/oact/ProgData/icp.html

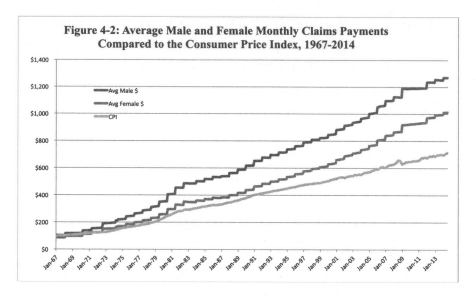

Figure 4-2: Average Male and Female Monthly Claims Payments Compared to the Consumer Price Index, 1967-2014

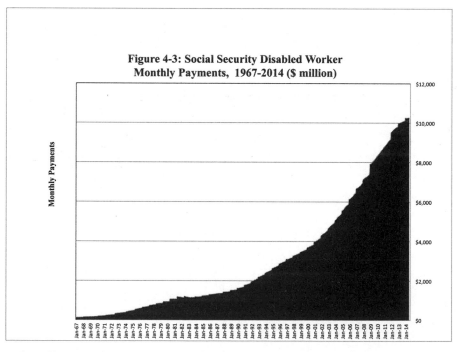

Figure 4-3: Social Security Disabled Worker Monthly Payments, 1967-2014 ($ million)

http://www.ssa.gov/oact/ProgData/icp.html

Professor David Autor of MIT has closely studied the SSDI system and its growth over the past few decades. For Professor Autor, this growth is rooted in the economic value of SSDI over most jobs that can be obtained by persons with neurological differences. The SSDI benefit is akin to an annuity; it's a guaranteed monthly income stream that lasts until death or retirement. This income stream is indexed to inflation and includes Medicare. The types of jobs available to most workers with disabilities do not pay wages much above SSDI; often do not include the health care coverage of SSDI; and most of all, do not provide the economic security of SSDI coverage.[23]

Professor Autor notes that several attempts have been made by the federal government to reverse the growth of SSDI. The most prominent of these has been the Ticket to Work (TTW) program designed by the Clinton administration and enacted by Congress in 1999.

TTW permitted SSDI beneficiaries to work for up to nine months without losing benefits and to continue to receive Medicare eligibility for up to eight years. Despite these changes, Professor Autor found that after its first decade in operation TTW failed to make a dent in SSDI rolls. Professor Autor reports, "fewer than 1,400 tickets (0.01 percent) of 12.2 million tickets issued in the first seven years of the program led to successful workforce integration." The economic incentives contained in TTW have not been sufficient to overcome the fear on the part of workers of losing the economic security of SSDI or the other obstacles to finding work in a competitive environment.

Several proposals have been put forward to reverse the rise of SSDI rolls and increase work participation. But none has gained traction, and none addresses the dynamics of autism unemployment and SSDI participation. Professor Autor has suggested greater financial incentives for employers to accommodate workers who become disabled and minimize the movements of workers from their payrolls onto the system.[24] But these incentives mainly involve workers who are employed and leave, largely due to physical ailments. They do not address the more common dynamic in the autism community of not having employment in the first place. Economist Mary Daly has suggested following those European nations, including the Netherlands and Sweden, that have responded to higher disability insurance rolls by shifting costs to employers and moving toward a private sector market for disability insurance.[25] However, the increased payroll costs for all workers are driving employers to hire less (and turn to independent contracting or demand more hours from their existing workforces). Adding more payroll costs with disability insurance should only accelerate these trends.

Among our Bay Area autism community, SSDI is a main form of income maintenance for the unemployed, along with Supplemental Security Income (SSI). Whereas SSDI requires some work history to qualify, SSI does not; parents and advocates, fearing long-term joblessness, will sign up young adults with autism for SSI when they leave high school. For the reasons set out by Professor Autor above, once on SSDI or SSI, recipients have economic incentive to remain.

The Evolution of Government Job Placement for "Workers with Disabilities"

Targeted government job placement programs for workers with disabilities have been present throughout the post World War II period. The current group of programs is more focused than past programs on inclusion in mainstream occupations. The programs are more targeted on the growing populations of persons with neurological conditions, especially autism.

Throughout the 1950s and 1960s, the government Employment Services sponsored initiatives to "Hire the Handicapped." Handicapped during these years meant mainly workers with physical disabilities, and the initiatives aimed at convincing employers that these workers were "no different" from other workers. Workers with neurological conditions, such as autism, were not yet part of the picture.

In 1955, the California Employment Service sponsored the Governor's Committee for the Employment of the Physically Handicapped, and in October 1955, the service participated in "National Employ the Physically Handicapped Week." The service's newsletter that month encouraged job service staff not to ignore the physically handicapped, since "denying employment to persons with physical disabilities who are able and willing to work is a glaring example of the ineffective use of manpower." Before World War II, the newsletter noted, disabled workers in the labor force were a rarity, but the past decade "has witnessed a gradual but nevertheless remarkable change in the picture." Of the 750 members of the Paralyzed Veterans' Association in Southern California, nearly half were "gainfully employed,"according to the newsletter. Singled out were the cases of a blind man repairing PBX switchboards at the Port Hueneme Naval Supply Depot and another blind man "expertly wrapping packages for export" at the Friden Calculator Company. The author concluded "the handicapped are performing commendably in practically every type of job or profession."[26]

By 1957, the service had adopted the slogan, "It's ability—not disability—that counts," and recorded 19,622 placements of physically handicapped persons in California during the year. The examples given in the service newsletters of 1957 chronicle the experiences of workers with physical disabilities, such as John R., "a public charge for a period following a hunting accident which caused the amputation of a leg." John was given "counseling to the end of providing him motivation to rejoin the labor force, and help in finding a job as an attendant in an animal hospital." Another example told the story of Mary B. The woman "crippled by polio, learned typing and shorthand, and she is working as an executive secretary in a busy insurance brokerage. 'Though she will be in a wheelchair for the rest of her life.' Her employer says, 'Somehow we have forgotten that she has any handicap at all.'"[27]

In the 1960s, the service broadened its job-placement efforts to include workers with nonphysical disabilities, including neurological conditions, mental illness issues, and mental retardation. Workers with these disabilities, though, were often seen as only fit for sheltered work-shops—distinct workplaces outside of the employment mainstream that undertook low-skilled repetitive tasks.

Inclusion of these workers into the employment mainstream grew in the 1970s and 1980s due to the passage of the Rehabilitation Act of 1973 and the emergence of the disability rights movement. Among government agencies, like the California Employment Service, workers with disabilities were now to be included in mainstream workplaces. Funds became available for aides, such as job coaches, to help with the transition. A network arose of community-based organizations that specialized in placement of the disabled.

The California Employment Service itself undertook job placement initiatives focused on inclusion. One of these, "Jobs for All," was launched in 2000, by the service with the California Department of Rehabilitation (DOR). The state unemployment rate was then down to 5.5 percent, among the lowest rates of the previous thirty years. "Jobs for All" combined intensive one-to-one job placement assistance with retention efforts, to continue at least two years following job placement. The program staff checked in regularly with employers to anticipate or address work-performance deficits.

Between May 2000 and April 2003, 2,487 participants enrolled in the program—a majority of whom entered on some form of public assistance. Nearly 42 percent were receiving SSI and/or SSDI upon program enrollment, and another 12 percent were receiving other public benefits, principally Temporary Assistance to Needy Families (TANF) and General Assistance.

A snapshot of the participants, culled from EDD records in April 2003, found that of the 2,487 enrolled up to that time, 1,106 had been reported as placed in employment and 563 employed at least ninety days. Of the 1,381 who had not found employment, around 400 had been dropped from the active lists as no longer looking for work and the remainder, around 1,000, were listed as still looking for work.

"Jobs for All" was designed as a pilot program to last over a period of years, with long term tracking of participants and their retention in jobs. However, the program was discontinued in 2004, after less than four years. The new state administration under Governor Arnold Schwarzenegger determined that the intensive and time-consuming placement and retention counseling had become cost prohibitive.

The job placements that were achieved in "Jobs for All" were primarily in lower level maintenance jobs, restaurant jobs, and office administrative jobs—the majority paying under $10 an hour. Further, nearly every placement required considerable time and attention by job counselors, walking participants through each step, personally contacting employers. The litany of things that could go wrong was long: missed or late appointments, failure to follow instructions, poor grooming, poor communication, and, most of all, work quality below that of other workers. Some work sites were patient with work deficiencies. Most were unforgiving and moved on to other employees.

Today, targeted job-placement efforts are underway throughout the United States by national nonprofits such as ARC and Goodwill and thousands of local job-placement providers. The programs often are funded through state departments of rehabilitation or federal disability funds. These targeted efforts generally utilize the same intensive job search assistance and follow-up as in "Jobs for All."

The San Francisco ARC, for example, serves persons with a wide range of disabilities such as cerebral palsy, Down syndrome, and wheelchair use. Like ARCs around the country, the San Francisco ARC has seen a sharp increase in clients with autism in the past five years so that now persons with autism form the majority of new clients.

For nearly forty-five years, from the 1950s through early 2003, the ARC operated a sheltered workshop, a separate workplace in which workers with disabilities performed basic tasks such as packaging and mailing. Today, the emphasis is on workforce inclusion.

Recent San Francisco ARC placements have been in supermarket chains, Safeway and Trader Joe's (clerk and bagger positions), retailers Noah's Bagels and Starbucks (maintenance, stocking), and the city's major law and advertising firms (facilities set-up and office support). Salesforce.com, the cloud computing giant, employs fifteen ARC placements, a mix of part-time and full-time, in facilities set-up activities.

With ARC's growing autism population, a good number of whom have college degrees, ARC staff hope to expand to a higher pay and skill level of job in these companies and others. But ARC is still searching to break through to jobs above the lower-wage and contingent positions.

ARC is the largest of the Bay Area job-placement entities for persons with autism and other neurological/physical conditions, but only one of the networks of providers. EastBay Innovations, Marriott Bridges, Toolworks, Community Vocational Enterprises, Employment Plus, and Jewish Vocational Services all provide targeted employment services to workers with autism and other neurological conditions.

Despite the growth of this government-funded employment network and its growing sophistication, it makes little more than a dent in autism unemployment today. Each placement requires a good deal of time and effort: contacting employers, carving out job placement opportunities, providing supportive services. Even when a placement is achieved, it is often part-time or of limited duration and it can (and often does) easily fall through.

The challenges in autism employment are more clearly evident as we turn to the recent job searches of a number of our job club members.

5

THE PERSEVERATIVE SCRIPTER AND HIS EMPLOYMENT SEARCH

THE BEST WAY to humanize and put in context the data we presented in the previous chapter is to describe in detail the background and employment search of some of our job club members. In this chapter, I start with an employment search I know best, that of my son William.

The oldest of our four children, William was born on September 8, 1989, and was diagnosed as being on the autistic spectrum shortly before his second birthday. For some years after he was diagnosed, I kept journal notes on his unusual behaviors as well as notes on the variety of therapies we tried. I also retained my correspondence with autism experts throughout the country.

The files are most heavy for his early years. The documents chronicle the attempt by my wife, Donna, and me to make sense of a neurological condition that was still little-known in the early 1990s. This is the story they tell of those early years.

William's behaviors parallel those observed in other children with autism: rigidity, routines, and distress when a routine is not followed, talking to self, flopping around. He must walk down the stairs in a certain manner, must follow the same order of activities at school, must watch certain videos or television shows in an order only he knows. At the park or at preschool, he rarely interacts, moving by himself according to his own rhythms.

We seek out specialists who are doing the early research and observation in understanding and treatment of children with autism. In 1994, I hear of promising interventions for educational and social gains, called Floor Time, being tested by Dr. Stanley Greenspan, and I meet with him in Bethesda, Maryland.[28] The following year I write to Dr. Oliver Sacks, whose book, *An Anthropologist on Mars,* details the amazing case of Stephen Wiltshire, an autistic young man in England with savant skills in drawing buildings and streetscapes with great accuracy after a single viewing.[29] Whenever I read or hear of new theories or therapies, I try to follow up, to find some way to keep William from drifting further and further from the shore, from us.

Among my early correspondences is one starting in 1993 with Dr. Thomas Sowell, a prominent economist at the Hoover Institution. Dr. Sowell in May 1993 has written a widely-distributed article, "Don't Let Them Put Labels on Your Children."[30] Dr. Sowell describes his son John, who didn't speak until he was almost four years old. Educators suggest to Dr. Sowell that John might have a form of mental disability. But Dr. Sowell does not accept this, and his article reveals that John recently received a degree in computer science and has become a chess master.

Dr. Sowell explains that "there is a whole class of boys who have exactly the same pattern of development as my son. It is an inborn pattern and usually includes special ability in math, music and memory. Over the years I have encountered two other little boys with the same pattern and was able to reassure their parents."

Dr. Sowell starts a discussion group among parents who contact him following the article. He asks us to write about our own experiences. In a letter dated August 28, 1994, I write the following about William:

> A few notes on William. He is now nearly 5 years of age. He goes to a special education program at the San Francisco Unified School district. William often stares out the window and talks to

himself, repeating verbatim scenes from Winnie the Pooh ("Oh Poor Bear, where are you?") or Thomas the Tank Engine ("I'm sorry I was so cheeky, said Thomas").

His behavior at the school is frequently odd and inappropriate. He does not interact much with other children: At the park he might go up and down the slide, talking or laughing to himself. He can go off like a roman candle if certain patterns are not followed. His tantrums at times can be so severe that he seems possessed. Uncertain what to do, Donna and I went early on to a child psychiatrist (God help us), to determine whether he was simply being willful or spoiled or something else was going on. Only after he was diagnosed did we come to understand the hard-wire issues.

At the special education class, one teacher and two teacher aides work with 12 students. William is one of two children on the autistic spectrum among the 12. The teacher and teacher-aides seek to reduce his withdrawal into his own world and into video-talk. They also seek to develop his ability to talk to and interact with other children.

In the afternoon, William attends various specialized therapies. Two days a week he works with a speech therapist. Two other days a week he works with a development therapist, to develop the social skills that come naturally to most children. A fifth day he works with a physical therapist on basic coordination and motor skills. He has swimming lessons on the weekends.

Today, William's speech remains very limited. He cannot respond to questions or comments made by other children or adults. If another child speaks to him, he looks uncertain and then may lapse into video-talk. His speech is often fractured and ungrammatical ("Sonia, what spells you?" if he is spelling her name or "No Sonia your sister," if she misbehaves.)

Through most of the day, a projector seems to be running in his head. While walking to Laurel Village or swinging on the bars at

Mountain Lake Park, he lapses into video-talk, reciting passages from "Arthur's Teacher Trouble," or "Beauty and the Beast" and laughing to himself.

Dr. Sowell later would capture stories of William and the other children in a book, *Late-Talking Children*, published in 1997.[31] Though Dr. Sowell's parents group disbanded in 1996, the Internet led to new groups of parents of children with autism, similarly sharing experiences and seeking answers, which Donna and I join.

Other journal notes from William's childhood describe his lack of engagement and our concern. A note dated September 17, 1995, describes his religious school class at Temple Emanuel:

> William goes willingly but seems completely lost. When the teacher calls his name during circle time, he does not respond, and only later when she moves on to other children does he talk to himself. While other children are doing crafts, he is singing to himself, "Jeepers Creepers, where'd you get those peepers" and repeating his videos. "What are you doing in my kitchen," he says out loud all at once while the teacher is discussing mezuzahs.

Two years later in September 1997, the inclusion teacher at his elementary school writes:

> William's lunch buddy program is going well. He has a different child sit with him at lunch in the cafeteria each day. Once he goes out on the yard, however, he is still playing by himself. That will have to be our next goal.

One strange behavior that we took some hope in, was his ability to watch a video or television show, and repeat it word for word. This *Rain Man* behavior is known in the autism literature as "perseverative scripting." From the age of three or four on, he could watch an episode of *Thomas the Tank Engine*, *Blues Clues*, or *Winnie the Pooh*, and repeat the episode word for word, even after one viewing. We saw in memory a skill that might be valued in school and beyond.

Power Rangers was his favorite show. He could watch an episode and then line up his Power Ranger figures and Zords and repeat the lines of each character, usually with proper intonations.

On Columbus Day 1999, William came downtown to my office for a few hours. A journal entry from that day notes: "He walks ahead, his shoes untied, his shirt partially unbuttoned, talking to himself, his hands flying out in strange movements, and skipping around to a beat only he hears."

At the office he takes out his Power Rangers and replays word for word a recent episode. When I try to move a chair, he says, "You can't move that, it's the megaship." He repeats word for word, character by character, an episode he saw a few days ago.

Autistic Behaviors Do Not Disappear With Time

We had hoped that his autistic behaviors would decrease over time. But this did not occur, not through elementary school and middle school, and not even through high school. He continued to talk to himself almost nonstop, to laugh out loud for no reason, to interrupt inappropriately. He displayed strange compulsive behaviors, had difficulty concentrating, and zoned out in educational settings.

We tried speech and developmental strategies recommended to us. We tried mainstream sports activities and specially targeted programs, including a drama program in Marin aimed at young people with neurological conditions. But none seemed to have much impact and especially the targeted programs seemed to have little value.

A note on April 1, 2000, describes an incident at the drama class performance. In the middle of the performance he interrupts to say, "All grown-ups and kids come to the stage; All grown-ups and kids come to the stage." The director tries to get him to stop but he ignores her and continues to shout. Only when the director stops the program and has everyone hold hands, does he settle down.

A month later, we visit Hollywood to show him the sets of his favorite shows, like *Power Rangers*. Our first stop is the Media Access Project, which places persons with disabilities in television shows and movies. William laughs to himself throughout the project presentation. At the next stop, the Hollywood Entertainment Museum, he interrupts a class to announce to the teacher, "So, what are you doing here?" When our guide whispers for him not to interrupt, he says loudly, "But I need to keep interrupting."

We visit Paramount Studios and meet with the president of Paramount. At this meeting, William begins laughing about something and can't stop. The president takes it in stride, though he seems more perturbed when William comments on the president's thin hair ("Why, your hair seems to be thinning, sir")—an observation that William has taken from his files of video-talk.

By the time he enters the San Francisco Unified School District in the early 1990s, the district has embraced the approach of inclusion. Throughout his childhood, William attends Claire Lilienthal Elementary/Middle School, a K–8 public school in San Francisco. At Claire Lilienthal, William is mainstreamed in a regular classroom and regular activities. He participates on the track team (mile run) and student government.

Upon graduation in 2004, he enters George Washington High, a 2,400-student public high school. At Washington High, William is involved in even a wider variety of activities. Along with track and cross country, he is elected to the student council each year and is a reporter on the school television station. (He hosts a segment, "Wow, That's Interesting," where he interviews students about unusual hobbies.)

Looking back, participation in these mainstream activities probably had more positive impact than any of the therapies or targeted activities. However, they did not eliminate the cognitive gaps or his compulsive behaviors.

One of these behaviors involves "counting cars." A journal entry of April 28, 2006, notes that Sal, one of the paraprofessionals at

Washington, observed William standing for ten to fifteen minutes on Geary and Thirty-Second Streets after getting off the bus in the morning. William was watching cars. Later William explains he is waiting for a red car to make a left turn on Thirty-Second. A few weeks later, William's sister, Anna, and I are worried when he is late coming home from track practice. We find him on the corner of California and Arguello Streets staring at cars.

Through high school, he does continue to show the unusual, even savant, skills of memory and calculation. He can multiply large numbers in his head. If you give him a date, say, March 12, 2017, he can tell you what day of the week it will fall on. He knows the order of United States presidents, their dates of service. He has lost none of his abilities to watch television shows and repeat them word for word, after one viewing.

"Parlor tricks," Donna and I sometimes say to ourselves about these abilities, since they are not translated into the classroom and have no clear applicability in work. However, we also know that in the highly specialized labor market of today, William does not need to be good at many things, only one thing.

For five years during William's youth, I am director of our California state labor department, the Employment Development Department. In 2001, I am contacted by Mr. Paul Orfalea, who is coming to Sacramento to advocate for inclusion in the workplace. Paul had started Kinko's copying in 1970 in Santa Barbara, grew it into a nationwide chain, and sold it in 2000, which made him very wealthy. In 2001, when he was coming to Sacramento to lobby, he was dividing his time between his business investments and his private foundation, which focuses on kids with learning disabilities—or, as he insists on calling them, "learning differences."

Paul is dyslexic, which was a big influence on his life growing up in Southern California. He was a terrible student and was in and out of schools and special-education programs. His main support was his parents, who told him he was not stupid or a failure. Now he spends time speaking to parents and teachers who work with kids with dyslexia or autism or other learning differences. His main message: These kids have a great deal of talent. They just have different learning styles. Don't let them be beat down by the school system. In the movie *Rain Man,* Raymond did have a severe disability and couldn't do a lot of jobs, but also he had unusual skills. Was his only choice between being institutionalized and living with his brother? Couldn't he have found a job using some of his amazing skills of calculation, for example, as an actuary?"

For a long time I took hope in Paul's comments and William's perseverative scripting ability. Surely this incredible memory could be put to some valuable use in the job market.

College Days

In 2008, William graduated from Washington High. He benefited from the academic supports available through the inclusion program. To a greater extent, he benefited from the inclusion community of teachers and paraprofessionals, who monitored his class progress and kept us in close contact. In his senior year we visited colleges in the Bay Area. We wanted him to live on campus, but be within an hour's drive. We decided on California State University East Bay (CSUEB), the state university school located on a hill in Hayward, about forty minutes from San Francisco.

He enrolled in the summer of 2008 to take the remedial math and English courses that were required of freshman who scored below certain levels on the entrance exams. He lived on campus. He struggled with these classes, but after two tries with the math course, managed to pass.

William's freshman year was also a time of new interest among the CSUEB president and staff in attracting students with autism. Then CSUEB-President Mo Quynami saw in the exploding autism demographics, both a potential market and mission for CSUEB. The Student Disability Resource Center (SDRC) had served students with autism in the past. Now a more structured project of recruitment, assessment, and academic supports, known as College Link was developed.

William was the sole participant in the 2008–2009 project development year, but groups of four to five students followed in the next two years. At the heart of College Link was an academic and social network: tutoring, SDRC supervision, and mutual support among students.

Among the students, parents, and SDRC staff, discussion soon arose on the extent of the academic supports and supervision, especially how much tracking and oversight the participants needed. SDRC staff envisioned a program, similar to autism programs arising at other college campuses, in which students had a regimented daylong schedule of tutoring and classes.

Though I was among the advocates of less regimentation and structure, there was no question that William needed far more structure than the average student. This came through a combination of tutors and my own oversight role. I drove to campus each weekend over the four years; checked in regularly with the tutors, even followed upcoming assignments and tests. I never worried about being a dreaded "helicopter parent," since I had come over the years to learn the different roles a parent must assume with different children.

Throughout the full four years, Donna and I had hoped to identify a subject area or skill that William excelled in (computer science, accounting, chemistry), but nothing emerged. He expressed interest in broadcasting, as a television reporter, and we thought, "Well it won't be long before persons with autism are in front of the camera." But while he was a reporter on the CSUEB television station, he struggled to research and develop stories. He expressed interest in becoming a filmmaker, but lacked skills in any of the areas of writing, computer animation, or cinematography.

Still he was able to graduate, with near a 3.0 average in interdisciplinary studies, a mix of theatre arts, communications, and general education. It was a down-to-the-wire process; he had failed a philosophy class and needed to retake it in the fall quarter of 2012. In the first week of 2013, though, we got word that he had passed, and was thus a CSUEB graduate.

Now for the hard part.

Search for Employment

William had been in paid and unpaid work settings since he was fifteen. In his high school years, he was an intern with Friends of the Urban Forest (planting trees), an administrative assistant intern with Jewish Vocational Services, and an intern at Zeum, the multimedia arts and technology museum. During the school year he worked part-time on weekends at Carl's Jr. in Daly City, cleaning tables and trays. Most of these he was able to obtain through work experience projects for youth with disabilities.

In college, the work experience projects disappeared and the summer work assignments became more difficult. During the school year, through the Student Disability Office, he was able to find a job cleaning tables at the Student Union and this lasted for four school years—due to a very supportive supervisor. One summer, we were able to piece together an internship at the California Department of Industrial Relations; another summer, an internship with the Department of Rehabilitation.

Prior to the summer of his senior year, we applied starting in January for five internships with nonprofits that were advertised at the University's career center. He did not receive one call-back. We then contacted twelve technology social media/Internet commerce firms in San Francisco, but did not receive any call backs.

Through a connection with the owner of a number of McDonald's franchises, William was able to obtain an interview and summer position as a crew member at a McDonald's in San Francisco. William was assigned to the lobby, to clean tables, organize and restock condiments, and greet customers.

He did fine on the greeting customers, but not so fine on the cleaning and organizing. He was compulsive about taking out of the trash anything that he thought could be used again. On several occasions, he was observed by staff taking partially used straws, napkins, and plastic silverware out of the trash for reuse. The regional manager talked to him several times, but like other compulsions, there is no logic. He was able to make it through the summer, but just barely.

In December 2012, following his completion of classes, he enrolled in the ARC of San Francisco employment program. ARC was willing to take him right away, which was important since without some structured activity, I was always holding my breath as to what he might be doing and how his behaviors, even innocent enough, might be interpreted. For example, he talked of going back to his former high school or even middle school, thinking that the students would remember him. But a grown man near high-schoolers or middle-schoolers is a recipe for misinterpretations. More generally, given his lack of guile, he was always a target for persons to try to take advantage of him, financially or otherwise.

ARC was able to place him within two weeks in a paid "try out" job with an advertising firm, Pereira O'Dell, to do hospitality setup, but this ended after two weeks. William has a phobia about dogs and there was a dog wandering around the premises. More generally, he is just not very competent in the hospitality skills of cleaning and stocking.

ARC then enrolled him in its classes on job search and social skills, and its adult day activities. William at least had somewhere to go each day, but it was no more than a form of warehousing. He had a college degree and was spending his day going on ARC adult day activities to the Exploratorium or Mission District or Ocean Beach.

In a few weeks, I came across an internship opportunity with Alameda County through East Bay Innovations, a nonprofit focused on workers with disabilities. The internship was part of Project Search, a nationwide program that provides unpaid internships with the promise of a path to paid full-time employment.

Generally speaking, unpaid internships are not a reliable path to paid employment, as employers often do not take these workers seriously or provide enough real work. Still, the opportunity to get William into a stable, large employer, with opportunities to move around, was very attractive. When an opportunity to join the program opened up, he applied and was assigned to the auditor's office. My hope was that we could find work involving, analyzing, or entering data that could make use of his calculation skills.

The administrative work turned out to be removing staples and checking numerical sequencing, and shredding and delivering mail. Worse, his job coach complained that the tasks were not being performed: he lost focus, stared into space, talked to himself, or needed to be prompted to undertake the work. His first job coach report on May 15, 2013, a month after he started, concluded, "He currently still has not mastered steps needed without prompting or cueing. The more difficult and hard wired habits seem to still need a constant stream of support to undo."

The next report, for June, added to the work complaints that he was arriving late to class and work numerous times: "Tends to lose track of time when he is eating breakfast at a nearby café or eating lunch in the classroom. William must be more aware of the time and give himself enough time to pack up."

In July, William was given a written warning that he was observed on five occasions on Facebook, in violation of Alameda County policy prohibiting use of social media sites. The following month he was given another written warning that he was observed at the worksite after 3:00 p.m., the formal end of work hours. On October 23, he was suspended for being on the worksite outside of approved work hours and also for storing food in his cubicle. The job coach wrote:

> When I went to check on Will today I saw that he had put a box of chicken wings behind his computer monitor—a common place he likes to store his food. I asked him if he could go put it

in the fridge in the break room. When we were alone in the break room I asked him about it and he said it was easier to take it to his cubicle than putting it in the fridge when he gets to the worksite. He then went on to say that it makes him uncomfortable to put the food in the fridge. He became upset, his voice was adamant, and his hands lifted and started shaking.

A few days later, he was let go from the program. The program manager wrote that the staff had learned of another incident: "He took a soda and chips from a fundraiser without paying for them [originally reported to us that he took a hot dog]." William appealed the decision on his own, but the program administrators held firm.

So we were back at square one, looking for a next option. The ARC itself was starting a Project Search program with the regulated utility, Pacific Gas & Electric (PG&E). PG&E has a workforce of 23,000 employees, primarily in California, including 5,000 in San Francisco. Like the Alameda County internship, the PG&E internship was unpaid, but held out the prospect of steady employment, with benefits. He spent a dispiriting two months back in the ARC adult day activities, wandering around the city. But in January 2014, he was able to start as an intern at the PG&E high rise at 77 Beale Street.

His first assignment was in the legal department. He had his own cubicle and computer monitor and the work tasks were mainly administrative: organizing and labeling files, delivering mail, and data entry. Some of the same issues arose again, regarding the ability to focus and undertake tasks on his own (as opposed to staring into space), the storing of food in his cubicle, and the taking of items from the trash.

A month or so into the program, we had a team meeting to go over how we could all "support Will," which mainly meant how we could get him to change his behavior regarding food. The job coach had written:

> Today, I discovered two pastries that were at least one day old hidden behind the boxes he was working on his desk. We have gone around and looked at other people's desks to show that the

53

only food people have on their desk is related to a break they are taking. He and I created the food rules together, which involve no food is allowed on my desk when it is not break time or lunch time, except coffee or a drink. He understands the issue but it remains a struggle to follow through especially when I leave him to work alone.

Following the meeting, the ARC assigned one of its behavioral therapists to help him address his food issues.

Project Search has interns switch departments after a few months. Will's next assignment was in the power generation unit. His assigned tasks again were mainly administrative, with greater focus on data entry and more challenging applications of Excel spreadsheets and calculations. This assignment went more smoothly, though the task management and food issues did not disappear entirely.

On June 13, 2014, Will and the three other interns "graduated" from the program. A festive reception was held at PG&E, at which several senior executives praised the "diversity commitment" of PG&E and the inclusion of the "PG&E community." However, paid positions at PG&E did not materialize. The following Monday, Will and the other interns were told to report back to the ARC for additional classes ("work preparation") and to await hoped-for placement. In describing Project Search, PG&E states that it will seek to transition graduates into full-time employment, but can make no guarantee.

Competition for almost all jobs at PG&E today is intensely competitive. For the skilled power positions, such as those that repair and maintain power lines or power generators, welders and linemen, PG&E is receiving hundreds of applicants for each position. It is also receiving hundreds of applicants for its clerical and administrative positions, including the huge billing and mailing operations in Sacramento. Mr. Rob Black, the PG&E community affairs manager, recalls, "On my first day at PG&E I went to the new staff orientation in San Ramon. Most of the people I met, in administration and especially in power line work, said they had been trying to get into PG&E for two to three years."

Ultimately, Will and the other interns will only succeed in getting and holding a job at PG&E if they bring value, if they can perform tasks as well or better than others. We are hoping that one of these tasks might be data entry, and perhaps other numerical analysis. Recently, we were informed that the customer service department is interested in hiring him for data entry, that a placement is likely "just around the corner." But a hiring document continues to elude us for now.

***

An update. It is now several months since the above was written. The PG&E hiring continued to be just around the corner, from June through September.

Finally, in September, we restarted an intensive job search and learned of a job order for an "office service specialist" (through Best Buddies, a job placement agency for workers with disabilities). The order was from Holland & Knight, a nationwide law firm with an office in San Francisco, and specifically asked for an adult from the disability community. Will interviewed and was hired.

He's been working there for two months. He works from 8:00 a.m. until noon each day. We are told that there is a good chance his hours can increase with performance. The Holland & Knight work culture is structured to try to make this placement succeed. Will's supervisor in office administration is repeatedly positive about having Will on board. The supervisor doesn't complain if Will takes time to master tasks or makes mistakes.

We haven't given up on PG&E for the long run. But for now, after two years of internships and programs, we're grateful for this.

6

EMPLOYMENT SEARCHES OF OUR
JOB CLUB MEMBERS

MY SON WILLIAM is in the early stages of his work life. Other members of our job club, though, have been in the job world for a longer period of time. Their experiences shed additional light on the employment dynamics today of the adult autism community.

Paul and Greg are two of our senior members. They both are college graduates, today in their fifties, who have been in and out of various occupations before settling in as self-employed handymen—though still trying after years to build viable businesses. Alex and Andrew are friends of William, in their twenties and early thirties, one working part time in recycling while designing pillow cases, the other a substitute teacher's aide in the San Francisco schools. Stacey, one of the minority of women in our group (only around 20 percent of adults with autism are female), has established a small pet-sitting business, while pursuing her goal to be a professional singer.

Among these members and others, most have some college education, even college degrees, though none is working currently in a position related to their education. Some have savant skills but have not been able to translate these skills into a work setting. Throughout their work lives, jobs have been fragile and often short-lived; and the employment process generally has gotten more difficult as they have gotten older. The worry, instability, inability to exhale never ends; though each has remained in the employment hunt, and none has settled for an existence of disability payments.

***

Paul Nussbaum, born in 1957, is currently writing an autobiography entitled *Conquering Aspergers—My Biography*. The existing manuscript is fifty pages single spaced and only covers his first twenty-eight years, to 1985. The manuscript starts: "I was born in April 1957, six weeks early and underweight for reasons unknown, in the San Francisco Bay Area. A few months later my family moved up to Napa, a short distance away, a small town at the time. I had Aspergers and didn't even know it."

Paul's description of his youth is of difficulties in keeping up in school and in fitting in with the other kids. "The public school I attended wanted to put me in a mentally retarded school and get rid of me. My parents would not have it and sent me to a private school instead. Whether it was accredited or not is questionable. The private school consisted of a husband and wife team of teachers, which ran the school out of their home on three acres out in the country."

After his parents divorced, Paul returned to the East Bay with his mother and graduated from El Cerrito High School in 1977. He went on to Contra Costa Community College and received an AA degree in 1979 and then continued at Sonoma State to pursue a career in geology. But he dropped out after the first year. "I had a very difficult time processing the huge volumes of information and making sure that I had all the information, which I didn't most of the time. It made doing the homework very difficult . . . at the end of the semester, I ended up flunking out of this geology program in a totally burned out state."

Paul returned to his mother's house in 1980, and through his former school, Contra Costa Community College, obtained a part-time job at a department store doing odd jobs. After a few months of irregular income, he started a neighborhood gardening, window washing, and rain gutter cleaning business. He distributed flyers around the neighborhood and actually obtained clients.

> Customer interaction was difficult at times, but the objective was straightforward—clean up the yard, which most of the time I could do, and once done, the customer was happy. I started my operation in early fall and it built up about a month or two later. I didn't get rich on it, but my financial situation was stabilized and I had money in my pocket. I felt a sense of accomplishment at this point. I looked at my skills and figured out a way to market them.

> The hardest challenge in my business was the communication and public relations with the clients. I would have to go around the neighborhood, going door to door and delivering flyers during the slow periods. I also had to do cold calls. This was my most dreaded task and I was overwhelmed when I would have to do it. I had to get over my fears and anxiety.

Paul continued the business until 1985, when he decided to try to join the Air Force, at age twenty-eight, and was accepted. His current manuscript ends at this point, with the concluding sentence "On to a new adventure."

Paul served in the Air Force until 1988, then returned to California and enrolled in Fresno State, where he earned a BA in geography in 1990.

He had one job related to geography, working for a map company as a cartographer, but this lasted less than a year. For the next six years, his work history is sketchy and includes a few short-term jobs mixed with long periods of no employment.

It was during one of his slow times that Paul's mom encouraged him to apply for SSDI. As part of the process, he went through a psychological and cognitive diagnostic process at the University of California, San Francisco. In 1997, at age forty, he received his first diagnosis of Autism/Asperger's Syndrome.

While the diagnosis did not alter his work situation, it did lead him to try to connect with other adults with autism. He joined a social group, Autastics, and after he appeared on a San Francisco State Autism panel in 1999, he became a founding member of AASCEND.

In 1999, he also decided to return to a business related to his gardening skills and expanded to include a variety of handyman home repairs. He relocated to Stockton and started "Paul's Handy Home Services: Handyman to Stockton, Lodi & Modesto." The business offers sixteen different home services ranging from indoor house painting to electrical repairs and waterproofing.

Paul continues to work in his home services business and at our job club meetings brainstorms with other members on marketing techniques. At the same time, he is involved in numerous projects. One of these projects is "Conquering Heights" a documentary film that discusses his mountain climbing accomplishments. Another is making presentations on adult autism. Paul has developed a flyer for himself as "Consultant-Presenter-Facilitator for Autistic People and Autism Service Providers." The flyer explains:

> Being diagnosed, at age forty, with Asperger's syndrome/Autism, after a long hard struggle with employment, academics and major communication and social issues, the light bulb went on—I learned about Asperger's and autism and found there was a huge population, just like me, with the same struggles. My focus is on helping others, including future generations, so that others will not have to go through the same intensive struggle that I went through trying to find their life path and niche in the world.

***

Andrew and Alex are two of William's friends at the job club. With a few other men with autism in their twenties and early thirties, they have banded together to go to baseball games and cultural festivals and concerts in Golden Gate Park and throughout the region. Often isolated before coming to AASCEND, they have become friends with their own small social network.

Andrew was born in 1981. Like William, Andrew possessed perseverative scripting skills at a young age. His mother, Camilla, recalls that he could memorize large sections of videos and repeat them word for word. He would insert them into conversations; "Adults found him charming," Camilla notes.

But early on his parents noticed "something was just not right." He did not interact with teachers. Enrolled at Presidio Hill, one of the better preschools in San Francisco, he lasted less than a month. He couldn't sit in a circle and participate. "We didn't know about autism at that time in the mid-1980s and thought that it might be a psychological or behavioral condition," Camilla recalls.

Camilla and Ron became part of a group that started a private school for youth with learning disabilities, which Andrew attended through high school. When Andrew was fourteen he received his diagnosis of autism, which was a relief to both him and his parents, in that it finally offered an explanation for his academic and social difficulties. After high school Andrew took courses at College of Marin and San Francisco City College, though he did not graduate from either college.

In 2000, a Workability program for adults with neurological differences, found him a file-clerk position at Bank of America. His job was to search microfiche files for canceled checks and gather information. He enjoyed this position; he saw it as a job in a professional environment that drew on his education. Camilla adds, "In all of the years since, he has never had a job that he was so proud of, and that made him feel he was contributing to a business"

Unfortunately for Andrew, microfiche was in its last stages in 2001. Within a year his job was eliminated. Then followed a period of short jobs, including helping out at Gold's Gym one day a week and volunteering at KQED radio and the Museum of Modern Art in the hopes of landing a position. The effort proved to be in vain.

In 2005, Andrew was placed through WorkLinks in a job with a plant nursery near the San Francisco Zoo. The nursery had a history of placing persons with neurodiverse conditions. Andrew helped with arranging and watering plants and with sweeping and cleaning. He worked there for two years before he was laid off as the Great Recession caused the nursery to cut back in staff. Camilla observes, "The nursery staff was really kind to Andrew; flexible and tolerant of differences. I don't think they wanted to lay him off but had little choice given the economic downturn."

On his own, Andrew went to a nearby nursery and asked for a job, and to everyone's surprise was hired. This position lasted less than a year. In Camilla's view, "The difference here was not the job responsibilities; these responsibilities were similar to the previous job. The difference was that the flexibility and patience of the first nursery was not present. Staff were either not willing or able to take the time for Andrew's training and mastery of tasks.

Since 2009, Andrew has been working two days a week in a recycling program with the city of San Francisco—one day a week at San Francisco General Hospital, another at the Municipal Railway barn. The latter is his preferred site since he enjoys wearing the Muni vest. (He thinks that people who wear vests have important jobs.)

The other three days a week, Andrew paints and sculpts at Creativity Explored, a program for adults with neurodiverse conditions, including autism. In early 2014 he sold a pillow design to Crate & Barrel's CB2 line—a line aimed at millennials that links products to compelling backstories. The design is now selling in Crate & Barrel stores nationwide—accompanied by Andrew's backstory. He hopes to sell additional designs.

The routine is not where he or his parents had hoped he would be in his thirties, but it is a step up from most of his twenties. Camilla's reflection: "I think he remains frustrated that he has never again gotten a professional job like the Bank of America microfiche file clerk job.

But for now, he has settled into it, and neither he nor we have given up on other employment. He goes regularly to the job club."

Like Andrew, Alex is in his early thirties and has gone through a variety of positions since college. He currently is a substitute paraprofessional in the San Francisco Unified School District (SFUSD), working on-call. He has been trying to move into a full-time paraprofessional position as a teacher's aide for preschool and elementary school students.

Alex grew up in the Bay Area, was diagnosed with a "learning disability" at age five, and attended a number of schools, including a boarding school in New York. He did make it through high school and spent three years at Monterey Peninsula College. He enrolled in the University of Arizona in 2003, but left after three years in 2005. His mother had purchased a home in San Francisco and he moved there in 2005. He enrolled in City College and then at San Francisco State University. At age thirty-one, he obtained a BA in child and adolescent development in 2012.

His work history in his twenties included short-term stints as a courtesy clerk at Safeway, as a busman with a coffee shop chain, as a video aide in the technology department of a major hotel, as a file clerk at a Xerox office. In each, the employer saw him as a step slow, became impatient, and let him go. He signed up with the Department of Rehabilitation and as part of his enrollment went through diagnostic tests, which led to his first diagnosis of Autistic Spectrum Disorder in 2011.

In August 2013, with DOR assistance, Alex was hired as a substitute paraprofessional with the SFUSD. The position is on-call: he does not know whether he'll be working until the morning. When he gets an assignment, he is sent to schools throughout the city. Still, it is the best job he's had. For the past six months, he's been trying to transition into a permanent paraprofessional position. He'd still be moving among schools, but would have guaranteed work.

The process has been a frustrating one, and as this is written in summer 2014 is still not resolved. He would email job club members from time to time during the school year, indicating how depressed he was about his work situation, how he had too much time on his hands, and not knowing each morning what he'd be doing. Other job club members have tried to keep up his spirits. They have written to SFUSD: don't only serve youth with autism but also hire from the autism community.

***

"Stacey's PuppyLuv" is a pet-sitting business that our job club member Stacey Kennedy started in 2011. In her early thirties, Stacey started this business after several false starts with other jobs. Like our other job club member businesses, it is modest in size (around four to five regular clients at any time), though Stacey's clear passion for animals may provide a driver for growth.

Stacey went through high school in San Jose and then spent two years at West Valley Community College and two years at Skyline Community College before leaving in 2003. Looking back, she thinks she lacked sufficient focus during this period and that her class selections were too scattered.

She had a number of short-term jobs as an aide to a Tae Kwon Do instructor and teaching English to senior citizens. For a good deal of the period from 2003–2011 she had no work, lived with her parents, and received SSI. She did begin to pursue an interest in singing, taking classes and looking for performance opportunities.

She was encouraged by her psychologist in 2009 to join a group of other adults with Asperger's syndrome, as a support mechanism to overcome discouragement. She sought out Autastics, a social group for adults with Asperger's syndrome, and through that was introduced to AASCEND at a picnic in summer 2010. She since has been active with AASCEND, singing at AASCEND events and joining the AASCEND board.

Her pet-sitting business was assisted by other AASCEND members in 2011, who became early customers. Her passion for the business is evident from discussions with her and from her website, which declares:

Stacey's PuppyLuv

I am pet sitter Stacey Kennedy.

I just love my puppies and they love me. My family has been in the Sunset area for generations. I will be happy to come and meet you and get to know your pets. We can then set up a schedule to care for them while you are away.

I have always felt an extreme affinity and closeness to my pets and animals and they seem to sense a kindred spirit in me. I have become involved in an ongoing study of pets, especially dogs and their daily needs. Within this, I have found a new skills at which I seem to be very good and which I love, that is caring for my pets and the pets of my friends. I just love making my puppies look their best.

Stacey has taken classes in dog grooming, and her business now offers pet grooming as well as pet day care, overnight sitting, in-house mail pick up, and plant watering. She recognizes that her prices remain too low ($20 a day for pet day care, $25 for an overnight stay), but she is reluctant to raise them.

At the same time, she is pursuing her dream of becoming a professional singer. She is currently performing in "The Barbary Coast," a community theatre production that has a six week run in a San Francisco bar. She is not being paid, but sees it as one route to reach her goal, adding that "I know how hard it is to be a professional singer, but am not ready to give up yet."

***

The job searches of our members should be put in perspective. Most non-autistic or "neurotypical" adults today mix periods of employment and unemployment. Non-autistic adults today face rejection from the great majority of jobs they apply for—and when they do find jobs, the jobs have less stability than jobs of previous decades.

Further, many non-autistic college graduates are working in jobs not tied to their education. A series of recent reports and news accounts have documented the high percentage of recent college graduates, at least 40 to 50 percent, in jobs that do not require college degrees.[32]

What is different for our members and other neurodiverse adults is the degree of instability and insecurity as well as lengthy periods of unemployment. The lack of work is far more prevalent, the firings more often, the disconnect between formal education and employment greater.

In the next section of the book, we examine the strategies now being tried to increase employment for adults with autism.

Part III
The Art of the Autism Job Coach

7

THE EVOLVING JOB WORLD WHICH ADULTS WITH AUTISM MUST NAVIGATE

AS IS TRUE of all workers, job counselors, and policy makers, adults with autism and their support teams need to be familiar with the main dynamics of our current job world.

Chief among these dynamics are three that guide us in thinking about employment strategies.

- Enormous job and worker movement—jobs being created and destroyed at a rapid pace and workers moving in and out of jobs.
- Heightened competition for each job opening.
- A breakdown in full-time employment and rise of alternative forms of contingent, part-time and independent contracting employment.

Taken together, these three job dynamics are creating a job world of enormous volatility, that places a premium on job search skills, as well as on abilities to adapt, pivot, gain new skills, and constantly look forward. Let's briefly consider each of these dynamics and their meaning for the autism community.

Enormous Volatility in Job Creation/Destruction and Job Turnover

Each month, the government announces official unemployment rates for the national, state, and local levels. Often these rates fluctuate little or not at all, suggesting little activity or change in the economy.

Yet, what these rates do not indicate is the high level of activity below the surface in the job market: jobs being added and subtracted, and workers moving among existing jobs. Each month in the United States millions of jobs are being created and millions of others are destroyed—even as the unemployment rate barely changes. Further, each month, workers are moving among jobs at an almost frenzied pace, with millions of individual instances of separations and hires.

Figure 7-1, based on employment data compiled by the United States Bureau of Labor Statistics (BLS), shows the private sector jobs created each quarter in the United States from 1992–2013. During this time the economy went through many ups and downs: the dot-com boom and bust in the early 2000s, the economic expansion of the mid 2000s, the Great Recession beginning in 2007 which continued through the first part of 2010. Throughout all of these times, even in the economic downturns, millions of new jobs were being created each month.

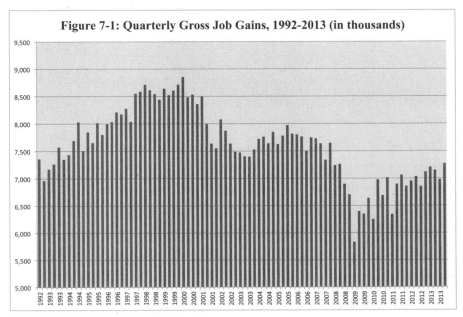

Figure 7-1: Quarterly Gross Job Gains, 1992-2013 (in thousands)

The job creation level reached a peak in the first quarter of 2000, when the number of jobs created averaged over 2.9 million jobs created per month. Even in the deepest throes of the Great Recession in 2009, though, job creation averaged over 2 million jobs per month.

On the other side, as shown on Figure 7-2, the same period of 1992–2013 that saw robust job creation also saw relentless job destruction. More than 2.8 million jobs were destroyed per month in the recession of 2001 and in the depths of the Great Recession eight years later. Even as the national economy was going strong, though, in the period of 2005–2006, an average of over 2.3 million jobs were being destroyed each quarter.

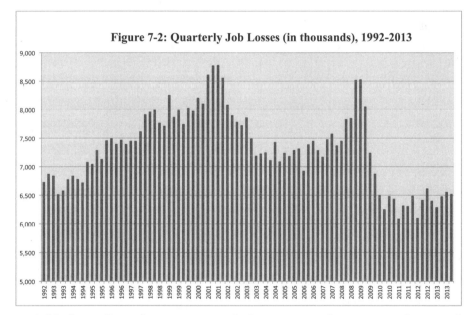

Figure 7-2: Quarterly Job Losses (in thousands), 1992-2013

Added to the job creation and destruction dynamic is the rapid movement of workers among existing jobs. Workers are moving in and out of jobs and the BLS tracks this movement each month as "Separations" and "Hires." Separations are jobs lost due to layoffs or discharges or voluntary quits/retirements. In most months over the past decade, more than 4 million separations occurred each month. Similarly, in most months over the past decade, a similar number of hires occurred. When the economy was relatively strong during the period 2004–2007, instances of new hires were over 5 million each month, and even when the economy sunk during the Great Recession, instances of hires ran 3.5 million to 4 million.

One impact of this volatility for all workers is instability of employment. Workers find themselves unemployed through no fault of their own. At the same time, the volatility also means constant hiring and a high number of job openings, at all times.

This is shown in Figure 7-3 below, which shows the number of job openings on any given day. The number of job openings on any day from January 2002 to January 2008 averaged over 3.5 million. It reached a high of 4.7 million job openings per month in March 2007, before falling sharply during the Great Recession. Even during the Great Recession, though, the number of job openings on any day averaged over 2 million. Since the Great Recession, it has begun its climb back to pre-Great Recession levels.

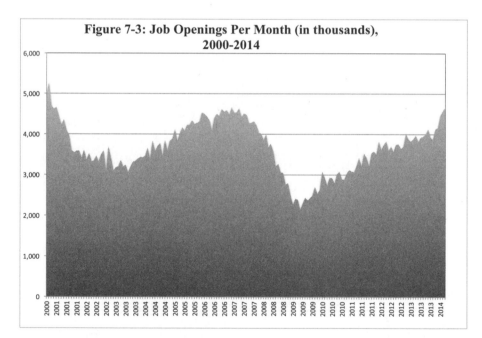

Figure 7-3: Job Openings Per Month (in thousands), 2000-2014

Greater Number of Job Seekers for Each Job

The enormous volatility of the American economy means on-going hiring opportunities accompanying the millions of job openings each day. At the same time, other BLS data on the number of job seekers in relation to job openings show how much more competitive the job market has become. This increased job competition started prior to the Great Recession, and has continued even as the economy has improved.

The BLS collects data on the number of unemployed persons per job opening. Figure 7-4 shows the number of unemployed persons per job opening from January 2000 through January 2014. At the start of the Great Recession, the number of unemployed persons per job opening, classified as actively looking for work, was 1.8. This number shot up to 6.2 unemployed persons per job opening during the Great Recession, before going down to 3.4 persons per job opening by December 2012, and to slightly more than two unemployed persons per job opening by mid-2014.

Figure 7-4: Number of Unemployed per Job Opening, 2000-2014

On the surface this BLS ratio of slightly more than two unemployed persons per job opening in 2013 does not seem to reflect a highly competitive environment. But economist Scott Winship of the Brookings Institute places the figure in a historical perspective. He notes that from 1951–2007, "there were never more than three unemployed workers for each job opening, and it was rare for that figure even to hit two to one."[33] Winship further notes that the increase in the unemployed per job opening predates the Great Recession. It increased during the recession of 2001 and failed to return to the pre-2001 level, even after the 2001 recession. Its "normal," non-recession level is evidently moving upward. Even after more than sixty months of expansion following the Great Recession, the number of unemployed per job opening is still greater than 2.0, above the pre-recession levels of 1.5 and nearly double the rate in December 2000.

Further, the BLS ratio of unemployed to job openings understates the heightened job competition in several important ways. The BLS counts as "employed" several categories of workers who are in tenuous employment situations, including the more than 8 million "involuntary" part-time workers and the more than 10 million independent contractors—a good portion of whom may be only nominally earning income. Further, the BLS ratio does not take into account the "marginally attached," the 2.6 million workers in January 2013, for example, who say they want a job but have not been actively looking the latest four week period. Factor these populations in and the number of unemployed/underemployed to job openings is significantly higher.

Most job seekers and job counselors sense a heightened competition for jobs today. The BLS data both provide statistical support and suggest the heightened competition goes beyond the Great Recession and current recovery.

Breakdown in Full-Time Employment and Rise of Alternative Forms of Employment

The third important employment trend of the past decade is perhaps the most important. It is the breakdown in full-time employment and rise of alternative forms of employment. These alternative forms of employment encompass the increase in part-time employment, the increase in temporary and permanent staffing structures, and the replacement of employment of any kind with the "gig economy" of individual projects and assignments.

The BLS counts part-time workers as "employed" for its unemployment rate calculation and for other rate calculations regarding employment. However, BLS also tracks part-time workers separately, and the data since 1990 show part-time employment (employment less than thirty-five hours per week) becoming an increasing part of the economy. Part-time work exploded in use during the Great Recession, rising by 3 million—especially "involuntary" part-time work—and has continued at these high levels since June 2009, the official end of the Great Recession, as shown on Figure 7-5.

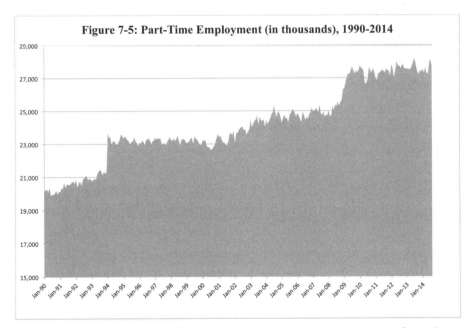

Figure 7-5: Part-Time Employment (in thousands), 1990-2014

Among part-time workers, there are major categories of workers who say they prefer part-time work to full-time work, including women and men caring for younger children or older parents, college students, and older workers. In August 2014, 19 million workers were "voluntary" part-time workers: working part-time and telling BLS researchers that they were not seeking full-time work.

The faster growth among part-time workers in the 2000s, though, has been among those who are "involuntary" part-time—they would prefer full-time employment but cannot find it. In August 2014, 7.2 million workers were working part-time, though they were seeking full-time work. This number was down from the high of 9 million involuntary part-time workers by the end of the Great Recession, but more than double the 3.2 million in the year 2000.

Part-time work has long been a part of the retail and hospitality industries, and in these industries, its use is increasing at the expense of full-time work. In fall 2012, labor reporter Steven Greenhouse visited a series of retail outlets in California and New York to chronicle this change.[34]

As Greenhouse noted, the retail/wholesale sector nationwide had seen its full-time job numbers reduced by a million full-time jobs between 2006 and 2012, while adding more than 500,000 part-time jobs. A specialist in retail consulting explained, "Over the past two decades, many major retailers went from a quotient of 70 to 80 percent full-time to at least 70 percent part-time across the industry."

Greenhouse went to Fresh & Easy, which bills itself as a socially responsible grocery company, as well as to Jamba Juice, the Express, Abercrombie & Fitch, and Bed Bath & Beyond. At all of these companies, he found workers on part-time hours with no set schedules. At a Fresh & Easy outside of San Diego, for example, a fifty-year-old worker oversaw seven self-checkout stations, and was constantly active in bagging groceries and explaining the checkout system. Yet, after five years, she remained a part-time worker, as did all twenty-two employees at her store. She earned $10.90 per hour, averaging twenty-eight hours per week.

While part-time work is heaviest in retail and hospitality, it now pervades all sectors and occupations. Its use has spread among occupations to include accountants, public relations professionals, even vocational job counselors.

Along with the growth of part-time employment has been the related growth of contingent employment—employment through staffing companies and professional employer organizations (PEOs). Staffing companies/PEOs enable companies to bring on workers without commitment to long-term employment, to gear up and down more quickly. Their growth reflects the reluctance of employers to make hiring commitments after the downsizing required during the Great Recession as well as the greater number of government regulations and costs on employers when they do hire today.

The staffing industry in the United States can trace its roots to the first years after World War II, but until the 1970s it was a very small part of the workforce. In 1956, there were only around 20,000 workers employed through staffing companies, mainly in clerical and factory positions, and by the early 1970s, the number was still at 200,000. Today, as shown in Figure 7-6, the number of workers employed through staffing companies is over 2.7 million.

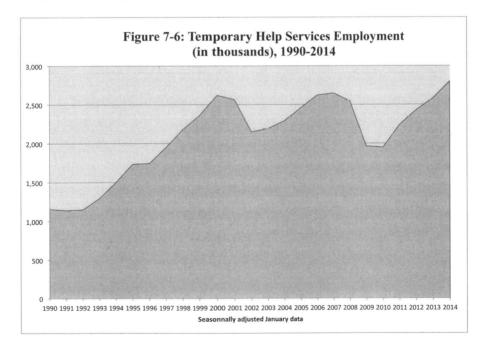

Figure 7-6: Temporary Help Services Employment (in thousands), 1990-2014

Source: U.S. Bureau of Labour Statistics

Similarly, the PEOs have grown into an industry of "employee leasing" in the past decade. The PEOs offer a leasing employment relationship or co-employment by which the PEO handles the recruitment, payroll, benefits, and performance management functions. By 2010, seven hundred major PEOs operated in the United States, handling payrolls totaling $81 billion. In the PEO structure, the worker is often a full-time employee with benefits. But the worker's tie to the primary employer is weaker than direct employment, and job security less.

Greater in number than part-time and staffing employment is the expansion in independent contractors. The independent contractor in many cases is even more contingent in employment and income than the others, generally having no guaranteed hours, no benefits, nor regular sources of work or income. In 1995, BLS identified 8.3 million workers as independent contractors and by 2005 that number had jumped to 10.3 million. In 2014, some estimate it at over 13 million workers.

The breakdown of full-time employment into these three forms of contingent employment reflects the rise of the project-based economy or the "gig economy" in the United States. Steady employment is replaced by employment based on assignments, individual projects, and forms of white-collar piecework. This is so across sectors and occupations, and including workers with advanced degrees.

Former *Vanity Fair* and *New Yorker* editor Tina Brown has lived most of her work life in a comfortable corporate bubble. But she cleverly captures this gig economy in a recent article describing how most of her friends, professionals with degrees from the most prestigious colleges, are now working freelance on multiple projects.[35] Imagining herself asking one of her friends, "So what are you up to these days?" she writes, "Well I'm doing two days a week, at, uh, this airline magazine, which is not bad because it allows me to still do my three days as, like, a consultant with my old company, where now you get, um, paid by the hour. Which works well, because you can even do that when you're traveling, which I had to do quite a bit of now because I'm also doing this speaker program for a tech company on the West Coast."

Brown adds, "For a while last year, the downsized people I know went around pretending they enjoyed the 'freedom' and 'variety' of doing 'a whole lot of interesting things.' Twelve months later, nobody bothers with that cover story anymore."

The breakdown in full-time employment did not start in the past decade. It has its roots in the late 1970s with the rise of the economic and social forces that began then to alter the United States economy—and that have increased in influence since. Chief among these forces: globalization, technology, the decline of private sector unions, and the changing work culture.

A proper discussion of these forces is beyond the scope of this book.[36] But a word might be added about the data on job tenure covering the period of the 1970s to 2006. Professor Henry Farber of Princeton University has undertaken extensive study of job tenure for the period 1973–2006. He examined data from twenty-one Current Population Survey supplements covering 876,063 workers and presented his findings in a 2008 paper, "Employment Insecurity: The Decline in Worker-Firm Attachment in the United States."[37]

Professor Farber found that for women in the private sector, job tenure did not change significantly. The decline in job tenure among women was offset by the sharp increase in labor force attachment among women that occurred at the same time, from the 1970s forward.

However, for men in the private sector the decline in job tenure was striking. The percentage of men aged thirty-five to sixty-four who had been with their employer at least ten years, declined from 50 percent to 35 percent. The percentage of men aged forty-five to sixty-four who had been with their employer at least twenty years, declined from 35 percent to 20 percent. Further, average tenure for men in the private sector dropped by nearly 25 percent in the 1973–2006 period.

Comparing the 1970s with the present, Professor Farber concluded, "The structure of jobs in the private sector has moved away from long term relationships." He added, "It seems clear that more recent cohorts of workers are less likely than their parents to have a career character-ized by a 'life time job' with a single employer."[38]

Adults with Autism Navigating in this Job World of Volatility, Competition, and Contingency

What does this new employment world of volatility, competition, and the gig economy mean for the autism community?

For adults with autism, as for all workers, it means changes in how to approach and find employment, retain employment, find other employment. Heightened competition for nearly all jobs means that adults with autism, like all workers, must be prepared to do far more than in the past in the numbers of job applications submitted and especially in the supplemental materials to these applications (i.e. in-house recommendations, videos, getting-in-the-door).

The volatility of job creation and destruction and worker movement means that adults with autism must be prepared to move among jobs. More than other workers, those with autism will seek more secure and stable employment situations. However, even these situations will not usually translate into lifetime employment. Adults with autism need the on-going networking and skills refreshment needed by all workers in the emerging job world. So too is the willingness to retool and be part of the retraining economy.

Similarly, the rise of the "gig economy"—the economy of project-based employment and independent contracting—requires all job seekers to be willing not only to move among employment situations but also to move between forms of employment. At some points in our work lives we will be able to find full-time employment; at other points we will need to be open to these other employment structures as we search for full-time work. Further, taking on project-based/contingent employment or independent contracting can often lead to full-time employment.

In the next three chapters, we will look in more detail on job search and navigation skills that adults with autism must have, and the accompanying role of the autism job coach.

8

JOB SEARCH MASTERY IN THE
INTERNET AGE

JOB-SEARCH STRATEGIES START with identifying job openings and smartly pursuing them. Today, the first step in the process often is searching the online job boards and online job sourcing that have come to dominate job search.

What is the best job board for job seekers today? For adults with autism? What is the best way for job seekers, including adults with autism, to get past the traditional gatekeepers and show their skills and job passions? Does the emerging technique of crowdsourcing represent employment opportunity for adults with autism?

This chapter sets out two elements of job search mastery: mastery of job boards and strategies of identifying/pursuing job leads, and mastery of the art of getting in the door. In the next chapter, we turn to a third element: the mastery of job networks.

Mastery of Job Boards

It wasn't too long ago that jobs were listed on 3x5 cards posted on bulletin boards at government employment offices and in daily newspapers.[39] While it is still possible to find a few job listings in newspapers, the larger job-search field has migrated to the Internet, with the explosion of thousands of job-search boards and job-search blogs.

The first major job boards appeared in the mid-1990s. CareerBuilder.com was one of the first, founded as Net Start in 1994 and selling software that enabled companies to list job openings on their websites and process responses. In the next few years, the company shifted to listing jobs on its own website, and purchased several competitor boards, including CareerPath.com and Headhunter.net.

CareerBuilder.com grew exponentially in the next decade, as did another job board launched in 1994, Monster.com.[40] Both continued to acquire competitors, add services, and diversify into new product areas.[41] By 2012, Monster.com had 1 million job postings on any day, and Careerbuilder.com an even larger number at 1.6 million job listings.

These job supersites have been joined by thousands of new job boards, with more coming online every week. These new job websites include job boards that focus on specific sectors, such as Dice on technology jobs and Absolutely Health Care on health care jobs, and job boards that focus on specific geographic areas. They also include the aggregators, also known as the mega-boards, Indeed.com and SimplyHired.com. These mega-boards collect and aggregate postings from Monster.com and Careerbuilder.com and other jobs and also from hundreds of thousands of employer websites.

The job boards enable job seekers to learn about thousands of job openings in their region in a fraction of time that was previously needed to go through newspaper listings (or 3x5 cards). They enable job seekers to submit applications and résumés with the click of a mouse, and submit hundreds of applications in the same amount of time that it once took to mailed or even fax a few résumés.

Yet, it is this same ease of identifying job openings and submitting résumés that has led the job search boards to be of limited value in job search today. When jobs are listed on job boards today, especially when they are listed on the major job boards, the employer receives hundreds of résumés or more.

Richard Bolles, the nationally-known career counselor and author, has turned his attention in recent years to online job search,[42] and is critical of much of the job board industry, referring to Monster.com and Careerbuilder.com as "stunningly ineffective" and "mostly a waste of time." Bolles argues that these supersites convince employers to pay for listings based on the breadth and traffic of the supersite, rather than any value to the job seeker or even to the employer. The sites also feature many companies that do not have real jobs but are seeking to sell services to job seekers or gather personal information for other purposes.[43] Bolles cites research that only 4 percent of job seekers who utilize the job boards ever find a job through the boards.

Bolles recognizes that job boards cannot be ignored but must be used smartly. What this smart use often will mean is augmenting identification of jobs through the boards with one or more of the following four strategies: (1) perfecting and tailoring the résumé; (2) researching the company prior to the interview, and identifying value added by your hire, (3) showing a passion for the job and competency by submitting materials to complement the résumé and/or interview; and of greatest value, (4) obtaining a recommendation from a current employee of the company. These strategies are not new. But they continue to be relevant in the Internet job age. Indeed, they are more relevant than ever.

Let's listen to two veteran job search experts on these strategies: Alyssa Gruber, executive director at Green Key Resources, a New York City headquartered professional recruitment and staffing company, and Marty Nemko, a prominent job coach in California since 1986. Gruber deals primarily in the very rarified world of hiring for hedge funds/venture capital funds and high level corporate offices—the executive assistant who earns over $100,000 a year, or the administrative assistant who starts at $50,000. Though her placement niche is office support, the job advice she gives is relevant to job placement at nearly all levels.

Gruber emphasizes that smart job board use starts with the résumé. The résumé is an extension of the candidate, a proxy for live presentation, the brand. It should be impeccable and follow the classic form (personal information, education, relevant work experience) with attention to content, clarity, and format. Cover letters are moot if the résumé is sub-par, and flowery cover letters are to be avoided. "The résumé can be likened to an audition," Gruber counsels. "You get one shot." She adds, "I'm often surprised how little time and energy is spent by the job seeker on the résumé, as it can be the most important chance to make an impression. A well crafted résumé, with succinct and clear articulation of skills and experience, can distinguish one candidate from the pool."

Gruber also has strong views on the interviewing process, as she explains: "So many job seekers don't take the time to learn about a company or think about how they add value prior to an interview. For any job, you need to go in and be able to explain how, with tens or hundreds of applicants, you stand out, how you can add value to the company. You need to be able to say, 'Let me tell you how I've been able to finish this project on a short deadline or the time I worked over the weekend to make a deadline or the project that was a big success for my company.'"

Marty Nemko is one of the deans of job coaches in California. He has been advising job seekers in person and through radio and news-paper columns since 1986.[44] He notes that in the 1980s a job seeker could send out a cover letter and résumé and get a response. Today, a job seeker needs to supplement job applications with additional efforts that show passion for the job and competencies.

If you're applying for a job in sales, Nemko recommends the development of a white paper with ideas for improving sales or improving operations.[45] Nemko explains, "For example, if you want to market fuel cells, write a paper called, 'The Seven Keys to Successfully Marketing Fuel Cells.' Send your paper to target employers and post it on your site or blog." Coaching a recent college graduate, Adam, who was seeking a job in the video-game field, Nemko advised him to go beyond submitting a résumé and prepare a white paper on successful sales techniques for video games. "Here's what I told Adam to do: Research and write a paper and call it 'Ten Video Games Whose Sales Exceeded Expectations.' The idea is to try to get the paper published. But even if it is not accepted for publication, Adam can mail this sample of his expertise to every marketing director he'd like to work for."[46]

Nothing is more important to a job seeker than a recommendation from a current employee of the company. In fact, with the overwhelming number of submissions through job boards, an in-house recommendation has become more important than ever.

A recent survey on the role of the in-house recommendation finds human resource officials using employee recommendations for more than 40 percent of hires.[47] The worldwide accounting giant, Ernst & Young, reports that in 2013, 45 percent of its non entry-level placement were through employee recommendations, up from 28 percent a few years ago and still below its goal of 50 percent. A recruitment official at Ernst & Young explains that in sorting among job applicants, "a referral puts them in the express lane." Enterprise Rent-A-Car hires nearly 40 percent of its workers through in-house referrals; Deloitte's percentage of hires from referrals is up to 49 percent.

A human resources consultant on the faculty at San Francisco State University identifies the referral as the most important search element. "You're submitting your résumé to a black hole," the consultant says of Internet job boards. "Whether it's fair or not, you need to have employees make referrals for you if you want to find a job." Of the supersites, the consultant adds, "We call it Monster.ugly. In the Human Resources world, applicants from Monster or other job boards carry a stigma."[48]

Mastery of the Art of Getting in the Door

Part-time and contingent employment and independent contracting often are not what most job seekers want. However, these alternative work arrangements can provide opportunities for creating a full-time job. The best job-referral is to start working with a company in some capacity and demonstrating ability. Mastery of the art of getting in the door, of leveraging these alternative work arrangements, is a second key form of job mastery.

BLS does not maintain data on the movement of part-time workers into full-time jobs. But job coaches point to part-time work as one of the best ways to connect with an employer, leading to full-time work. The avalanche of résumés brought by the Internet places a premium on the worker who is known by an employer.

Being hired on a project basis or as an independent contractor is an alternate means of becoming known to an employer. The labor market in the United States is distinguished by movement among forms, from employee to independent contractor to employee to contingent work, several times over a work life. Workers move among different employment forms, and no worker is locked into a form.

Taking up contingent or project work or working as an independent contractor does not consign workers to these forms of work forever. It's important to view work done on a non-employee basis as a possible path to full-time employment rather than as a permanent destination.

Volunteer work can also lead to full-time employment. Job coach Nemko encourages volunteering in order to get in the door, but within certain parameters. The worker who is volunteering should have clear understanding from the employer that she or he won't be left sitting around but will be integrated into the company operations. Further, the volunteer should have a strategy going in on how the volunteer work might lead to a job at this firm or another firm.

Internet Crowdsourcing to Find a Job

Beyond the job boards, the Internet is creating other job placement techniques, including crowdsourcing to find a job.

Crowdsourcing is the process by which the Internet facilitates communities of individuals coming together to address social or economic issues. Cooltown Studios, a blog devoted to crowdsourcing, defines it as "the act of taking a job traditionally performed by a designated agent and outsourcing it to an undefined, generally large group of people in the form of an open call." Wikipedia is perhaps the most well-known crowdsourcing platform: individuals do not go through an admissions process or hiring process to participate in Wikipedia.

Crowdsourcing is finding its way into the job training/placement world through three avenues. The first is through Internet sites that allow persons to compete on design projects or other tasks. For example, an employer may post a request for a logo design or request a solution to a problem with an app. In response, individuals voluntarily offer their ideas and labor. Employment may result for one or more of the individuals through providing the "winning" solution or through meeting other prospective employers or partners through the crowdsourcing exercise. Alternately, the participating individual may benefit in a job search from showcasing problem-solving skills, "Especially in the tech industry, employers want to see skills applications rather than traditional résumés; show, don't tell," notes Ms. Kris Stadelman, director of the NOVA Workforce Investment Board in Silicon Valley.

A second approach is through crowdsourcing a job announcement or even developing the requirements for a job announcement. Companies are using social media, especially Twitter, not only to announce job openings but also to seek ideas through crowdsourcing for the job description. A third approach of crowdsourcing for employment is a variant of this approach: job seekers are using crowdsourcing to obtain leads for their job search or to critique their résumés, including video résumés.

Crowdsourcing as a job strategy has its proponents, including Ms. Stadelman and Professor Panos Ipeirotis of New York University. "Crowdsourcing is the new interview" Professor Ipeirotis declared in a posting last year.[49] Professor Ipeirotis celebrates the absence of the traditional interview process, and the fact that with crowdsourcing the evaluation is being done on the job. "The selection of the best participants happens naturally, without the artificial introduction of a selection process mediated through an interview," Ipeirotis states.

It is too soon to reach conclusions about crowdsourcing as a job-search technique. Its weaknesses are clear: for the employer it can be an overly complex way of recruiting, and for job seekers, it often can be an investment of time that is ultimately not remunerated. At the same time, like the other Internet economic activities, it breaks down traditional barriers to entry and eliminates the traditional gatekeepers.

Internet entrepreneurs are creating job-search products and bringing them online regularly. Within the past few years, new Internet-based businesses have come online that help people find internships, complete online classes tailored to individual employer job applications, or find volunteer work that will lead to full-time employment. Job mastery will mean keeping up with the rapidly evolving tools available on the Internet.

It should be noted, though, that no development in the Internet job age has reduced the importance of the most basic job search skill: self-knowledge. Even in the Internet age, the job search starts with identifying individual job skills, sector interests, and preferred workplace environment and interests. Richard Bolles' best selling job search book, *What Color is Your Parachute?*, first published in 1970 when 3x5 cards were being used at employment departments, had as its central theme the self-inventory of skills and workplace preferences.[50] This self-inventory continues to be the starting point for any job search today no matter what the Internet technology involved.

9

JOB NETWORKS AND MUTUAL SUPPORT

OUR AUTISM JOB Club is only one of hundreds of job clubs throughout the United States: voluntary groups of mutual support and extra-governmental networks. For some time, job clubs and job networks have been central concepts in job placement. Even in the Internet age, their importance is only growing.

The Hidden Job Market and Mastery of the Job Network

The best-known part of the job market is jobs filled through public job listings. However, a larger part of the job market consists of hires made without the employer's running a job listing, or listing a job simply for show, after a candidate has been identified. This larger segment is often termed the "hidden job market," and is estimated at over 50 percent or more of jobs.

Mastery of job networks and job clubs enables workers to access this hidden job market. In the hidden job market, a worker can identify a job opening before it is posted and gain an advantage in securing the job—even if a posting is subsequently made as part of a required process. Additionally, in the hidden job market, a worker at times can convince an employer to make a hire, even if the employer had not previously planned to add staff.

The hidden job market is highlighted by two experienced career counselors who specialize in this market: Dan Asher, author of *Cracking the Hidden Job Market*,[51] and Duncan Mathison, author of *Unlock the Hidden Job Market*.[52]

Mathison estimates the hidden job market at 50 percent of all hires during better economic times and up to 70 percent of all hires when the economy is down. "In tough economies, employers spend less on recruiting. As a result, more jobs are filled that are not publicly posted." Mathison notes that in networking there may be six degrees of separation, but "most people never get past two (a friend of a friend), so networking efforts will peter out. Why? Because people have to care enough about you and your job search in order to introduce you to their best connections." Mathison puts forward two strategies for expanding the job network: (i) don't restrict networking contacts to professional contacts—"everyone you know should be aware of your search," and (ii) "create a list of organizations you think hire people like you and share the list with everyone in your network."

Similarly, Asher urges job seekers to utilize a job network broadly understood; not only family, friends, and former coworkers, but also acquaintances in dance groups, bowling leagues, religious organizations, and even casual contacts. "You get jobs by talking to people, so your goal is to talk to a lot of people," Asher explains.

Asher cites the case of a technology executive who had been unemployed for a year but didn't tell any of his friends or former coworkers. The executive applied for over thirty jobs online but had no success. Asher convinced him to be upfront about his job search and talk to as many people as possible. The executive did find a job with a startup, based not on a formal job listing but on a lead from an acquaintance.[53] Asher explains, "The hidden job market is a job you can't see . . . If I can hire somebody without posting the job, I'm going to do that 100 percent of the time. Given the choice of sorting through hundreds of difficult-to-distinguish applications and taking the recommendation of a contact or considering an applicant who has demonstrated initiative and enthusiasm by getting in touch directly, most hiring managers will take the most efficient path."

The Job Club and Mutual Support

In the emerging job world, voluntary job networks and mutual support, outside of government, will expand. Many of these job networks will be of family, friends, acquaintances, and former coworkers as at present. Others will be formed through online connections.

The job club is an established form of networking and mutual support that will see its role expanded. Job club members usually do not know one another beforehand. They come together freely to share leads, serve as job coaches to each other, and most of all to try to help each other out of the isolation of a job search.

The job club as a job search strategy of mutual support has existed for several decades and in a range of settings, both public and private. Job clubs are sponsored by the Workforce Investment Boards administering federal job training funds, community job training groups, veterans groups, fraternal organizations, and industry associations. They are sponsored by churches and synagogues (though in synagogues there are sometimes two job clubs, so congregants can say, "That's the job club I don't go to.").

The State of California labor department since the 1980s has sponsored "Experienced Unlimited" job clubs, and there currently are twenty Experience Unlimited job clubs throughout the state—in Fresno, Torrance, West Covina, and Irvine to name a few. Job club members are given office space in the state offices and staff assistance, but mainly are encouraged to take ownership of the process, including volunteering time on the job search process of others as well as their own.

ProMatch is one of the most well-known job clubs in California. It is located in the Silicon Valley and is operated by the state of California and the local Workforce Investment Board, the NOVA Board. It has roughly 200 members at any time, heavily tilted toward laid off technology workers in their thirties and older.

The job network is the central concept of ProMatch. ProMatch tech job seekers are encouraged to start with their own family/friends/acquaintances and then to seek contacts from each other and from ProMatch alumni. ProMatch has a LinkedIn page for job contacts among members and from previous ProMatch members who have found employment.

Kris Stadelman is the executive director of the NOVA Board, and a strong proponent of both in-person group and online group job networks. Regarding the job club in-person, Stadelman notes that in today's job world, it is easy to feel that a job placement will never occur, that hiring or even serious interviews will never happen. ProMatch celebrates each job interview: "ProMatch above all is about giving job seekers hope," she says.

ProMatch encourages its members to take advantage of the online job groups, especially LinkedIn. All ProMatch members are encouraged to participate in LinkedIn and be active in the job associations and industry associations on LinkedIn. Further, they are encouraged to continue to be active on LinkedIn even after they find a job, for advancement opportunities, for any future times of unemployment, and for providing contacts to current ProMatch job seekers.

Connie Brock is a NOVA job coach who oversees ProMatch. She came to job coaching in 1997 after a career in finance and after retraining for a job-counseling degree. She has worked with thousands of clients, especially tech workers in the Silicon Valley, both at NOVA and through a private job coach practice.

Brock emphasizes the role of the job club in combating the isolation and discouragement of the job search as well as providing a structure and accountability. She recently hosted one of the semi-annual ProMatch alumni events where over 130 former ProMatchers now employed came back to connect with current members. Ms. Brock describes videotaping ten of the alumni on why they came back to help:

> The response was pretty unanimous—ProMatch let me know I wasn't alone. ProMatch helped me develop the confidence to sell myself. ProMatch helped me get clarity and focus. ProMatch provided me much needed support and accountability. The point is that looking for a job is lonely and it's too easy to go to all or none thinking, foreclose on options, make bad decisions, not have a sounding board or interview practice opportunities.

Beyond ProMatch, Brock advocates job clubs in other affiliation groups, such as religious and service group networks. Writing about a woman in her early sixties who had been laid off in 2008 as an executive assistant at an advertising agency, Brock recommended:

> I would encourage her to contact local churches in her community to see if there is one that has a job search support group. If not, I would recommend she think about getting a church or local chapter of a service organization to support her in starting one as a way to help her and others facing similar challenge. I would put her in touch with an organization like Menlo Park Presbyterian's Career Actions Ministry or Cupertino Rotary's Job Club to get ideas/information about how to get one started.

Like others at NOVA, Brock is a proponent of the online job network, as well as the in-person job club. She encourages all clients to build an online network, particularly utilizing LinkedIn.

The Internet Job Networks

In just the past five years, LinkedIn has come to dominate the online job networks and play a prominent role in various stages of the employment process, from getting a job, to advancing within a company, to moving among companies and sectors. In the first quarter of 2009, LinkedIn reached 27 million registered users. By 2013 the number of registered users was over 200 million worldwide, of whom 74 million were in the United States.

LinkedIn was started in 2003, not by professionals in the workforce community but by technology entrepreneurs in Silicon Valley. Reid Hoffman and other founding members of LinkedIn had developed PayPal, the industry leader in enabling people to transfer money securely over the Internet. Hoffman also had developed Socialnet, an online dating service, and was an early investor in Facebook and Zynga.

LinkedIn includes some job listings. But its main function is as a professional networking site. Users are encouraged to upload a résumé and profile that sets out their expertise, professional interests, and professional accomplishments. Users develop a list of "connections," other LinkedIn users whom they know, especially in a professional capacity. Users are encouraged to contact their connections regularly to discuss professional issues and business opportunities. Users are also encouraged to join the various LinkedIn "groups," online associations of LinkedIn users of similar occupation (accountants, high school instructors, social media specialists), sector (health care, leisure and hospitality), academic, or corporate backgrounds. Over 500,000 "groups" currently exist on LinkedIn.

Hoffman's 2012 book, *The Start-up of You*, includes one of the finest discussions of networking and the hidden job market today.[54] Hoffman argues that job networks need to be cultivated throughout a work life, not only in times of job search. Job networks need to be nurtured and expanded on a daily or weekly basis. With an effective online job network, the worker will learn of job opportunities before they are posted and will be able to find in-company contacts for referrals when jobs are posted.

As the title of his book implies, Hoffman asks all workers to regard themselves as start-ups. Like a start-up, the worker cannot be passive, waiting for someone to hand him a job or become complacent in a job. He must identify ways he can add value to an enterprise and do so during his employment. Further, like a start-up, he must adapt to changing economic conditions, refreshing skills and learning new ones. Whatever job security existed in the past is now largely extinct and job insecurity will define the future.

The worker today must define himself as being in "permanent beta," continually adapting to economic change. The online job network is a means of keeping on top of the change and being ready to move upon job loss.

As a company, LinkedIn has maintained its dominance by adapting and changing over the past decade. For example, it continues to add new ways for a user to research companies for future employment, apply through LinkedIn for jobs with the user's LinkedIn résumé and presentation materials, and add blog postings with the LinkedIn profile.

LinkedIn has not only become the favorite of workers, but also of employers and employment recruiting firms. A significant portion of LinkedIn's revenues comes from recruiters who pay for access to the LinkedIn data of users and résumés, and who use LinkedIn to identify candidates for job openings.

Other online job network sites have emerged to challenge LinkedIn. Facebook and Twitter are other Internet networking sites that have far more users: in April 2013, Facebook had 750 million unique monthly visitors, Twitter 250 million monthly visitors, and LinkedIn 110 million monthly visitors (among its 200 million registered users). Yet neither Facebook nor Twitter has shown anything close to the understanding of the job network and hiring process that LinkedIn utilizes.

Neither has become a threat to LinkedIn in professional networking. Facebook is offering BranchOut as an attempt at the job network market. But so far it has failed to attract attention among job seekers or recruiters, hindered by Facebook's role as a non-business network.

The Challenge to Those Who Lack Networking Skills

"What three words of advice are job seekers most often given? Network, network, network," notes job coach Marty Nemko, adding, "Problem is, increasingly that's bad advice."[55]

Nemko argues that while a majority of job seekers may find jobs through networking, a large portion of the workforce is not adept at networking. Nemko extends this lack of network skills to his clients and readers: "I bet you don't (have the networking skills); if you did, you probably wouldn't be reading this job-search advice column." He advises this network-challenged group to focus on competently pursuing the public job leads.

Across the labor market, a quarter to a third of workers do not have strong networking skills. They lack the skills of reaching out to others in person or online, to strategize, to size up opportunities and individuals, to confidently ask for a job or an assignment. This is true of most of the members of our Autism Job Club.

But this does not mean the job network, in person or online, is not applicable to those without networking skills. It means that these job seekers, particularly in the autism community, will benefit from the assistance of family and community networks, and from the autism job coach. In the next chapter, we explore the role of the autism job coach, which includes facilitating job networks.

10

THE ART OF THE AUTISM JOB COACH

J AN JOHNSTON-TYLER AND CINDY Zoeller are artists when it comes to autism job coaching. They employ the smart use of job boards and emphasize the importance of getting in the firm door, job networks, and other strategies set out in the previous two chapters. They teach, modify, and adapt these strategies for their job seekers with autism, and, most of all, assist with implementation.

***

Johnston-Tyler is the founder and CEO of EvoLibri, a firm that she started in 2007 in Santa Clara, California. EvoLibri now serves around 100 clients at any time, nearly all of them adults with autism.

Johnston-Tyler came to Silicon Valley in 1962 when her father took a job with Ampex, a company manufacturing recording devices. Her first career was in the technology field and by the 1990s, she was a mid-level manager and business lead for electronic publishing at Cisco Systems (following stints as a technical writer/manager at Hughes LAN Systems, DHL Systems, and Juniper Networks). Her son was diagnosed as being on the autistic spectrum, which led her into the autism world, and a career change.

> He was diagnosed with Asperger syndrome when he was four and it was a new diagnosis to psychologists so people didn't really

know what to do about it. Being a problem solver, I figured out what would help him. As I did that work I realized, wow, there are services for little kids and school-age kids, but nothing for teenagers and nothing for adults. So I thought it would be interesting to see what kind of services would help them.

Johnston-Tyler received a master's degree in counseling. She wrote a book, *The Mom's Guide to Asperger Syndrome and Related Disorders* and launched EvoLibri.

EvoLibri offers counseling for personal relations and communications and it hosts social groups for persons on the spectrum in Silicon Valley. Job placement, though, has become its main service, reflecting the hunger for employment for adults on the spectrum, even in the Valley's robust economy.

Johnston-Tyler and the job developers on her staff use each of the main job search and placement techniques used by effective job coaches/job developers for workers without autism. They try to make smart use of job boards, to perfect and tailor résumés, to convey a passion for the job targeted, to obtain a recommendation from a current employee of the company targeted. They utilize a "getting in the door" strategy of part-time, contingent, and volunteer work; and use job networks, traditional, and Internet networks.

However, they also modify these techniques—herein lies *the art of the autism job coach*. They assume a greater role in contacting potential employers, walking the client through the application process, assisting the client in drawing on networks, and serving as an intermediary with the employer after placement. They are sensitive to the value of disclosing the client's autism prior to the hiring process, but also aware that some clients prefer not to disclose. Ms. Yvette Analla, one of the EvoLibri job developers, explains: "In many cases, we disclose prior to the interview because if we don't, the interviewer is just going to wonder what's wrong. In these cases, I may go with the client to the interview to educate the employer on job coaching and retention services."

In job placement, EvoLibri starts with an assessment of the skills and interests of the individual. Following Temple Grandin's dictum on skill diversity among adults with autism, Johnson-Tyler emphasizes that although adults with autism are often spoken of as one group, they differ widely in abilities and interests. For example, technology jobs often are singled out as jobs for persons on the spectrum. Yet, Johnston-Tyler explains that less than a quarter of her adults with autism are interested in a technology career, or show any aptitude— "Graphic arts, daycare, retail are all fields job seekers are interested in, and show aptitude."

Following the individual assessment, EvoLibri staff design an individual employment program. To the greatest extent possible, EvoLibri staff try to find a competitive advantage of the client: a skill or character trait possessed that enables the client to perform as well or better than other applicants. Such a skill or trait cannot always be identified, but this is the goal. The individual employment program then might aim for direct job placement or it might aim for a more indirect route through part-time, contingent, or volunteer employment.

On the job search process, EvoLibri staff use job boards but don't rely on them. Johnston Tyler explains:

> We encourage our job seekers to learn about job boards, and have a drop-in application morning each Wednesday when we help job seekers put in applications and maintain an electronic record of all the places they are applying to. Craigslist, Indeed, and Snagajob are some of the main boards we use, though there is no right board. However, job boards for all workers, non-spectrum as well as spectrum, bring few placements. So our job applicants particularly can't put too much stock in them.

Most job placements at EvoLibri come about through the job developers contacting employers and developing a placement, usually with a job coach for some period of time. If a placement is not possible, then other forms of work or volunteer activity are tried. Most of all,

EvoLibri seeks to get their unemployed clients out of their houses and into some activity right away. Johnston-Tyler adds:

> What we are determined to avoid above all is for the job seeker to stay at home, play video games, become more depressed and discouraged. Direct job placement is the goal, but getting into an activity, unpaid or volunteering, is a baseline. Almost always, if you get out there in some positive activity, skills will be gained, good things will happen. Avoiding isolation and depression is true of all of us, but especially true for our autism community.

Yvette Analla, aEvoLibri job developer, illustrates the company's approach with two recent clients. For each, the process starts by attempting to identify a trait or traits that will give the client a competitive advantage. For one client, it proves to be a skill with car detailing, for the other, a background in chemistry. Analla assists in résumé writing and interviewing, but as a *job developer* she goes beyond this and actively seeks out and negotiates with employers.

In the case of the first client, Analla discloses the autistic condition, which she regards as key to the placement. Here are her notes on the process:

> Male, age 26, diagnosed with high functioning autism very early. Client has job services funded in part by the California Department of Rehabilitation (DOR).

> Client has very narrow interests—cars being one of them. He has been detailing cars for neighbors and people he knows since he was a teenager. Client came to EvoLibri for job development services after he finished with his training for employment. Work was done with the client on interviewing techniques and appropriateness of behavior. A résumé was created and references identified. The job search was based on his interests and a job at a major car manufacturer as a car detailer was identified. Job Developer

helped client with the application process and then contacted someone in HR at the company.

Analla told the recruiter about his abilities *and* disclosed his disability. She scheduled an interview and instructed the client to research the company ahead of time. She accompanied the client to the first interview. She reported that her client "did a great job." Her client impressed the interviewer with the facts he knew about the company and about the car models. The client knew every model, their features, when they came out, and where they were manufactured.

Had the recruiter not known about his disability, Analla believes it would have been unlikely that her client would have gotten the second interview. Analla also informed the recruiter about her job coaching and the continuation of her coaching even after placement. Analla's client got a second interview at the job site (a car dealership), and she accompanied him to this interview as well. Her client was hired at a pay rate above the minimum wage. As of this writing, Analla reports that he has been employed for six months. However, his employment has not been free of problems. For example, he

- doesn't want to detail the white cars, only the black cars;
- he sometimes gets hung up on looking at the features of the cars and stops working; and
- he sometimes just shuts down and won't talk to anyone.

Analla notes that the client's employer has been flexible so far with the client's behavior but she can't be certain how long that will last. She sees a need for some form of on-going therapy regarding the client's rigidities—though such therapy is beyond EvoLibri's contracted services.

Analla's second client did not want to disclose his autism, which limited her role and the job development provided. Here are Analla's notes:

Male, age 25, diagnosed with high functioning autism.

He has a BS in biology and biochemistry from a University of California campus. He was in special education classes until high school where he was mainstreamed. He endured bullying and teasing "but got through it." Most recently client has received certification as a Pharmacy Technician and that is his job goal.

The client went through Workplace Adaptability Skills Training (funded by DOR) at EvoLibri, where he learned appropriate workplace behaviors and worked with the job developer on his job search. The job developer used traditional job-search techniques, including applying for jobs online through regular channels. The job developer assisted with drafting cover letters, identifying appropriate job leads, and practicing interview skills. This client did not want to his autism disclosed, so the job developer was limited in follow up.

The client took some temporary jobs that were not a good fit and then accepted a seasonal job at a retailer of software, consumer electronics, household appliances, and computer hardware. He stayed for about four months and continued to apply for jobs as a pharmacy tech. Just recently, he was hired as a pharmacy tech trainee at a major drug store.

Johnston Tyler observes that this client did not have the same competitive advantage in passion/background for the selected occupation as the first client. But one competitive advantage of this second client may be his predisposition toward accuracy and honesty—"Not a person who will be stealing drugs." Indeed in a number of occupations in which honesty is an important characteristic, the competitive advantage of the adult with autism may be this honesty and an accompanying unwillingness to cut corners.

Another autism job coach artist, Cindy Zoeller, is the facilitator of our Autism Job Club. She also has a private practice in job placement focused on adults with autism. Her approaches are similar to those of EvoLibri.

Zoeller spent more than a decade as a job/career counselor, first at two vocational colleges (Universal Technical Institute, DeVry Institute of Technology), and subsequently in private practice. In 2007, she joined a vocational career counseling group in Sacramento that was beginning a focus on adults with autism. Since that time, she has worked with hundreds of adults with autism and has become immersed in the autism community.

Zoeller uses job boards with her clients, but mainly as a way of learning about the types of jobs available and identifying employers whom she might contact for her clients. Zoeller's experience is that only a very small proportion of persons on the spectrum can effectively use job boards or job networking on their own. Assistance can come from family or friends or a volunteer job coach or a paid job coach. But left to their own devices, persons on the spectrum usually flounder using the conventional job-search boards and processes.

As does EvoLibri, Zoeller tailors the job search to the individual worker's interest and abilities in a four-step process she calls "Customized WorkForce Planning," aimed at not only finding a job, but developing a career path.

- Step 1 is occupational exploration, often using one or more written occupational assessment tool, and highlighting strengths of the job seeker.
- Step 2 is any additional education needed to support a career path; the education may be through a formal community college or private post-secondary school or it may be through the educational offerings available online, such as Coursea and Khan Academy.
- Step 3 is an associated internship, paid or unpaid, to gain experience.
- Step 4 is the pursuit of employment, "teaching and practicing all of the classic job search techniques known to prepare any job seeker for searching and interviewing," according to Zoeller.

In the pursuit of employment, Zoeller works with each job seeker to prepare a résumé and practice and re-practice common interview questions (i.e. "Why should you hire me?" "Why do I want to work here?"). She works with the job seeker to identify openings and prepare applications. Once an opening is identified, she will not rely on the general résumé submittal process. She will contact the employer and pitch the skills of her job seeker.

Zoeller encourages her job seekers to try for a full-time job, if that's their goal. But she also encourages them to get in the door not only through paid or unpaid internships, but also through part-time and contract employment. Beyond these four steps, Ms. Zoeller identifies a further job search element as perhaps the most important: whenever possible, utilizing the network of family and friends to identify and pursue jobs. She urges her job seekers to let all family and friends know about the job search. She actively reaches out with the job seeker to family and friends, including pursuing employment in companies that family and friends work in.

> The first way that family and friends can support the employment quest of their spectrum family member or friend is to be an advocate for employment within the very companies that they, themselves, work in. They know this person well, know what their strengths are and what they're good at doing. Talking to their own employers and carving out a job description could be a very successful endeavor.

Beyond the direct employers are companies that family and friends might have contacts in and can help either identify job openings, listed and not yet listed, or perhaps even carve out a position.

> Applying through job boards brings a competition to be the best candidate for the job. Often that is not on paper and in interviews the person on the spectrum. We may know that this person has the potential to become an excellent employee, but to stand out enough to be selected for an interview—solely off of an application and a résumé—against the often times hundreds of applicants for the job, hasn't typically happened in my experience.

Zoeller sees the traditional low-tech networks of family and friends as most effective for persons on the spectrum. But she also encourages job seekers to participate in the online networks, especially LinkedIn. Zoeller has all of her clients set up a LinkedIn account and take time and effort in doing so. She does not expect her job seekers will find much through the groups and associations on LinkedIn. But in her experience, potential employers often examine LinkedIn so that not being on LinkedIn can be a red flag to employers.

The specialty of the autism job coach or counselor is a growing one, following the growth in number of adults with autism. Within our Autism Job Club, the past year has brought new autism coaches as volunteers.

John Comegys is one of these volunteers. Like Jan Johnston-Tyler and Cindy Zoeller, Comegys did not set out to be an autism job coach but has found himself drawn to the autism community. He graduated from Pacific University in Oregon in 1973 and had a lengthy career as a teacher and vocational rehabilitation counselor before deciding a few years ago to be a job coach for adults with autism. He drives from Dixon, California, each month to assist in job club activities. He uses many of the same skills he gained as a vocational counselor, but modifies them to address the additional level of services needed by most of our adults with autism.

For all of the autism job coaches, the issue of when and how to disclose the autism condition is a main challenge. Jan Johnston-Tyler notes that some job seekers (like the EvoLibri client mentioned above) do not want to disclose and thus the coach must respect this choice. She further notes that publicity linking the Sandy Hook Elementary School shooter in 2012 with Asperger's syndrome has given some pause about disclosing.

Yet on balance, she and the other coaches urge being upfront with an employer about the condition. This directness helps identify employers who affirmatively want to hire persons with autism—often because of a connection to autism through family or friends. More importantly, it helps to avoid disappointment and job dysfunctions that are likely to arise down the line if both sides don't know what they're getting into.

In March 2014, I received an email from Dr. Norman Hearst, a family physician and researcher at the University of California, San

Francisco, whom I had not heard from in fifteen years. His son Max and William had been classmates at a preschool program for children with autism. Max, now twenty-four, had graduated in late 2014 from the University of California, Riverside, with a degree in chemistry. For the past thirteen months, though, he has been out of work and largely isolated at home. By Norman's count, Max has submitted over forty résumés online but has received only two or three interviews.

I suggested that Max come to our Autism Job Club to join our broader autism community and that he contact EvoLibri, since Yvette Analla is located in the East Bay. Additionally, I suggested that Norman might identify some of his contacts in the Bay Area's biotech industry. We discussed Max's hesitancy to disclose his autism and agreed that this hesitancy impedes most job placement—"Any interviewer can look at Max and know something is off," which is what I would say of William and most of our job club members.

Norman expressed a criticism of autism job counseling that I have heard from many of our parents and members: too much advice on how to get a job, not enough job contacts. Max is a Department of Rehabilitation client and has received advice on his résumé and interviewing and job boards, but not job interviews.

That's why I suggested EvoLibri. Jan Johnston-Tyler and Yvette Analla will pick up the phone and call employers and pitch Max's skills and desire to work to the employer. They will do so understanding the concerns of the employer as well as Max's needs. This is part of their autism job coach artistry.

In late 2012, job coach dean Marty Nemko came to speak to an AASCEND meeting. As he detailed in a subsequent post on his blog, he came away "exhausted." He had come to the Job Club thinking of "Aspies" as highly skilled, if socially awkward. Instead, he reported that one person couldn't remember his name, another said he was so exhausted at a job interview trying to appear normal that he "was useless for three days" and a third "slipped into a mystical foreign language mid-sentence." Nemko concluded that most of those in attendance had anomalies severe enough to make it difficult for them to find stable employment in today's job market.

A number of the AASCEND members were upset by this post. But his account did capture the challenges for many adults in finding employment, and he's certainly not incorrect that it can be an exhausting pursuit. Further, his post highlighted that most important quality of an autism job coach: patience.

Additionally, within a short time, Nemko began to take an interest in autism employment. He periodically sent newspaper articles to the group that he thought would be helpful, and showcased autism employment several times in 2013 and 2014 as a topic on his weekly radio show. He began to work in his private practice with job seekers with autism. In his avocation as a keyboard player, Nemko joined with one woman with autism who aspired to be a singer, to develop a "Musical Tribute to Autism" that they performed at local clubs. In describing the performance, Nemko wrote of the woman, who found a day job as a research assistant, "As a young child, they called her retarded. Then they called her shy, very shy. Then she was diagnosed with Asperger's. Now they call her amazing."

A River Runs Through It—Helping Those Closest to Us in the Job Search

A main theme of this chapter and the previous two chapters is the active involvement of family members and others close to the job seeker in job search. This is true for all job seekers but especially for adults with autism. However, a word in this addendum about approaching job search for those closest to us.

Near the end of *A River Runs Through It*, Norman Maclean's novella of a family in Montana in the early part of the twentieth century, the author's father reflects on his adult son, Paul, who has failed to live up to his promise.[56]

"It is those we live with and love and we should know who elude us," the father, a Scottish Presbyterian minister, says. Paul is an expert fly fisherman and fine writer, but cannot avoid the gambling and drinking that leads to his death. His brother and father want to help him, but do not find a way to do so.

So it can be in trying to help those closest to us in their job searches, especially friends and family. We want to be of assistance. But we do not always know how to do so. We ask ourselves, What is the right approach? How can we help others avoid the mistakes we've made? How can they profit from our experiences?

Job coach Nemko has addressed this challenge over his decades of practice. He has developed an approach applicable to all job seekers, including adults with autism.

As Nemko explains, "First, start the conversation. If you wait for the job seeker to do so, you may be waiting for Godot." In *A River Runs Through It*, Paul's drinking and fighting are not openly addressed. A loved one's job search can be an awkward topic, but avoiding it is rarely the best approach.

Second, telling someone who is struggling what to do rarely succeeds. "Nobody wants advice. Giving advice is not empowering. Rather than say, 'I think you should do *x*,' you might say to a family member or relative, 'Tell me about what you'd like to do, if anything.'" Again, listen to their words.

Third, if the job seeker doesn't come up with sufficient ideas on his or her own, put forward specific offers of assistance. "Is there any part of your career search in which I can be of assistance to you? Can I help with job leads, a fresh pair of eyes on your résumé, help to gather additional career information?"

"If the job seeker is stuck, you might inquire, 'Do you want to mainly work with your hands, in office administration, with people? Do you want to work in a large or small company? Do you want to start your own business?'"

Fourth, if the job seeker is following a route that appears unrealistic or illusory, don't hesitate to urge reconsideration. "You might say, 'I can understand why you'd want to do this, but might you want to consider other paths, other ways of pursuing your interests that involve, say, less risk.'"

With a smile, Marty Nemko calls his approach, "California Coaching." He has found it to be more successful than trying to tell someone what to do, especially a family member or friend.

None of us should worry these days about being too involved with the job searches of family and friends. To their regret, Paul's brother and father stood back from getting involved in his life. We don't want to make the same mistake. We will want to act, if we can assist in the job searches of those closest to us.

"I am haunted by waters" is the well-known final line of *A River Runs Through It*. However, equally poetic and relevant in job search is the previous paragraph:

"Eventually, all things merge into one, and a river runs through it. The river was cut by the world's great flood and runs over rocks from the basement of time. On some of the rocks are timeless raindrops. Under the rocks are the words, and some of the words are theirs."

Part IV
Autism, Technology, and the Growing Internet Economy Employment

11

AUTISM AND THE TECHNOLOGY ADVANTAGE

IN THE PAST few years, employment in the technology sector has been a focus of autism employment activity among advocates for people on the spectrum.

The focus has been especially intense on quality control and data-conversion jobs. Autism-employment advocates have made pilgrimages to software testing companies in Western Europe employing adults with autism. Companies that engage in software testing and data conversion have been established in the United States, with a main goal of employing adults with autism. Seminars have been held claiming unique technology skills of adults with autism.

So, what have we learned about autism and technology employment?

Specialisterne and the "Dandelion Philosophy"

In June 2011, an article appeared in the *New York Times* about a Danish company that was formed to directly employ persons on the autistic spectrum in software testing, quality control, and data conversion.[57] The article rapidly careened around autism websites and blogs. It generated a great deal of hope relating to technology as a field for employment of persons on the autistic spectrum.

The company, Specialisterne, was founded by Thorkil Sonne, whose son, Lars, was on the autistic spectrum. Sonne's professional background was in Information Technology; he'd spent fifteen years with telecommunications companies in Denmark. He became active with Autism Denmark and became convinced that persons on the autism spectrum could undertake IT tasks with greater skill, concentration, and attention to detail than the general population. Specialisterne was launched in 2004, with a mission of employing persons on the autistic spectrum. The larger goal was to demonstrate the employment possibilities the field of technology affords to workers on the spectrum.

By 2011, as the *New York Times* reported, Specialisterne was thriving. The company had won contracts for software testing and data conversion with major Danish and global firms, including Microsoft and Oracle. It was employing over fifty persons on the spectrum.

Sorkil's "dandelion philosophy" of autism skills captured the imagination of the autism blogosphere. Sorkil explained that a dandelion can be seen either as a weed that invades a garden or as a valuable herb, with medicinal qualities. "A weed is a beautiful plant in an unwanted place," Sonne explained to the reporter. "An herb is the same plant where it is wanted. Who decides if something is a weed or an herb? Society does." For autism advocates, the message became: recognize the skills in technology and put them to use.

Sorkil parlayed the *New York Times* article and other publicity to launch an autism employment operation into the United States. He caught the attention of Delaware Governor Jack Markell and received a $200,000 grant from Delaware-based Longwood Foundation for a Specialisterne-like operation in the state. He relocated to Delaware aiming not only to start a company but also to start a Specialisterne movement in the United States creating tens of thousands of jobs.[58]

Specialisterne Offshoots in the United States

Other software testing companies soon arose in the United States, inspired by Specialisterne—and by another Western European company employing persons on the spectrum in quality control jobs, Passwerks in Belgium. The U.S. companies included Aspiritech in Illinois, Semperical, and the Specialists Guild in the San Francisco Bay Area, and ULTRA Testing in New York.

Aspiritech in Highland Park, Illinois, was one of the first of the autism-focused software testing firms in 2009. It was founded by Moshe and Brenda Weitzbeg after their son, Oran, thirty-two, was let go from a job bagging groceries. It drew inspiration from Specialisterne and set out with the slogan "Software Testing Harnessing the Power of Asperger's Syndrome." The motivating idea, similar to Specialisterne's, was that persons on the spectrum possess the traits for excellence in software testing—*intense focus, comfort with repetition, and memory for detail.*

Media accounts of Aspiritech in 2011 presented the five Aspiritech testers on the spectrum as colorful characters, with various characteristics of autism: Katie who talks nonstop, Brian who hates driving, Jamie who is bothered by bright lights and vacuum cleaners, Rider who draws cartoons of himself as a DeLorean sports car, Rick who doesn't like to sit near other people. Like other adults with autism they had characteristics that got in the way of mainstream employment: social awkwardness, poor eye contact, being easily overwhelmed by tasks. But these characteristics did not prevent them from being skilled testers.

In its first years, Aspiritech did obtain software testing contracts with technology companies. A representative of one company, HandHold Adaptive, praised Aspiritch, saying "There is a pride in their product you don't usually see in this type of work." Aspiritech soon was cited as a model for starting similar businesses throughout the United States. "There have been a couple of attempts in the United States, and Aspiritech is the one that's making it," explained Scott Sandifer of the University of Missouri, one of the nation's experts on autism employment.

In the San Francisco Bay Area, two software testing companies employing persons on the spectrum were launched in 2012: the

Specialists Guild and Semperical. Like Aspiritech, the Specialists Guild (the Guild or TSG), was founded by parents of children on the autism spectrum, Luby and Andy Aczel. Andy Aczel brought to TSG over thirty years of experience in the fields of software development and networking, primarily in Silicon Valley. He had been involved in a series of technology start-ups, including as vice president of engineering at Silicon Spice and Premisys and CEO of Packet Island, a cloud-based tools company acquired by Broadsoft.

In the Silicon Valley economy, Mr. Aczel saw software testing work frequently outsourced to offshore companies. He was convinced that a software testing firm operating in the Bay Area and utilizing the focus and concentration skills of persons on the spectrum, could be competitive with the offshore companies by keeping costs low and eliminating distance and language barriers. From the start, the Guild was intended to serve as transitional employment, providing training and work experience for young people on the autism spectrum and allowing them to move into jobs at larger tech firms. The Guild adopted the following statement of purpose: "Our motto—Focus on Ability—reflects our goal to help individuals on the Autism Spectrum and companies to achieve mutually beneficial employment relationships by bridging the gap of misunderstanding that surrounds people with Autism in our society."

The Guild started with three trainees in February 2012 in a classroom donated by Jewish Vocational Services, in a four-month training course taught by Andy himself. By Fall 2012, another four trainees had been added. Since the Guild had no real capital to hire staff, Aczel also did the marketing, seeking unpaid as well as paid testing contracts—both of which were slow to come in. Luby Aczel handled the administration and grant writing.

Down the road in Palo Alto, three high-level tech veterans in 2012 were envisioning and planning a much bigger software testing enterprise than the Guild. The founders of Semperical, Steve Perricone, Sundar Raj, and Rick Reddy, all had major roles in previous tech start-ups and connections with the venture capital firms of Silicon Valley. Perricone, the founder and CEO, had been involved in five start-ups, most recently as the CEO of a cleantech company, BioFuelBox—a firm featured at the Davos Economic Forum of 2010.

The Semperical founders visited Specialisterne in Denmark and Passwerks in Belgium, where they met with autism experts. They were passionate about their employment mission and about the unique testing skills of persons on the spectrum, explaining in early promotional material: "Our specialized program unleashes the incredible natural talents of engineers on the autistic spectrum. Customer testimonials show that, on average, engineers with those qualities deliver twice as fast with double the accuracy of their neurotypical counterparts."

In late 2012 Semperical announced the goal of employing more than 300 persons on the spectrum in the next few years. It envisioned a structure that could employ persons on the spectrum nationwide by enabling them to work at their homes or remote sites throughout the United States. Like Aspiritech, Semperical was held up as a breakthrough in autism employment and replicable model.

Specialisterne and Similar Companies Struggle to Find a Market Role

Despite early hopes of ground-breaking success, by 2013, Specialisterne, Aspiritech, and Semperical were all encountering difficulties as market-based businesses.

From the start of the publicity surrounding Specialisterne in 2011, autism advocates had raised questions about the company's claims and its viability in the United States. In Denmark, Specialisterne had received generous wage subsidies for workers with disabilities provided by the government of Denmark. The Specialisterne publicity did not mention these subsidies, but they were a key to the financial health of the business.

Indeed, once established in the United States, Specialisterne soon abandoned plans for a software testing business. Instead, it assumed a more conventional job-training and placement role in recruitment, assessment, and training for other software testing companies. Mr. Sorkill still spoke of a revolution in autism employment and creating thousands of jobs for adults with autism in testing. He argued that the "the potential market is enormous as the corporate sector is challenged by a huge lack of talents in the area of science, technology, engineering and math."[59] But Specialisterne quickly abandoned its role of a business creating these jobs. Without the wage subsidies that it had received in Denmark, Specialisterne was not willing to go forward as a business entity. Aspiritech continued to train and employ workers on the spectrum throughout 2013, though by the end of the year it had not yet become a self-sufficient business. Its business revenues covered around half of its operating budget. The remainder of the budget came from contributions from foundations and individuals.

Semperical was unable to get off the ground. Two of the three founders left and Mr. Perricone found himself unable to obtain the private financing for his plan of offsite software testing by adults with autism.

The company piloted an online training program in software testing for twelve adults with autism in fall 2013. The participants were located throughout the United States. The testing was set to the International Software Testing Qualifications Board standards and Semperical reported eight of the twelve successfully completed and demonstrated tester skills.

However, no hires were made. Within a short time, by the end of 2013, Semperical formally shut down. Mr. Perricone continued in 2014 to pursue his vision of an autism-focused testing business, though as of this writing no business has been launched.

With more modest goals, the Guild was able to show some placement results in 2013. It managed to place two of its testers in temporary positions at Salesforce, a leading developer of cloud-based enterprise software. Additionally, Mr. Aczel was able to generate a small amount of paid software testing work to give two other testers some paid work experience.

The autism-focused software testing firm that reportedly is succeeding best as a standalone business today is ULTRA Testing in New York City. It was founded in 2012 by two experienced technology entrepreneurs trained at MIT, Rajesh Anandan and Art Shectman. They independently had arrived at the same conclusions as the other testing entrepreneurs noted above: the competitive advantage afforded by adults with autism in software testing and the opportunity for a software-testing business employing these adults and based in the United States. "There is a tremendous untapped talent pool right here in the United States," Anandan explained. "Of the 2 million Americans with Autism Spectrum Disorders, 85 percent are not employed. Yet, at least one-third of this population are high functioning and have heightened abilities matching the exact skill set required for software testing—focus, attention to detail, natural pattern recognition ability, intelligence, and curiosity."[60]

ULTRA combines its ten testers with neurotypical (non-autistic) project managers. "We're in a highly competitive industry, so the only way we're going to succeed is by delivering consistently superior results for our clients," according to Anandan. "And we're unlocking an incredible talent pool to do just that."[61]

Software Testing Jobs in Major Software Companies

While the autism-focused software testing businesses have struggled, another employment strategy has gained momentum. This strategy involves placing adults with autism as software testers in established software companies. The movement is being propelled by parents who work in these companies and by the perception in these companies that adults with autism do have advantages as testers.

In 2013, the international German software firm, SAP, announced an "Autism at Work" initiative. SAP at the time employed 65,000 workers, and announced it would start aggressively recruiting adults with autism to join its workforce, especially in tester jobs. Its stated goal was that 1 percent of its worldwide workforce (650 workers) would be adults with autism by 2020.

Jose Velasco, parent of two children with autism, is the head of the SAP autism initiative in the United States. The initiative started up in 2014, with four sites, including one in Palo Alto. Seven adults with autism were recruited and trained in spring and summer of 2014 and placed in SAP jobs at the SAP Palo Alto facility. A second cohort of seven adults is scheduled for training in Palo Alto in 2015.

Mr. Velasco explains that adults with autism tend to pay great attention to detail, which may make them well suited as software testers or debuggers. In addition, "they have a very structured nature and like non-ambiguous, precise outcomes. We're looking at those strengths and looking at where those traits would be of value to the organization."[62]

Beyond the job of software tester, SAP is looking at other positions that might be good fits for adults with autism—in business procurement and manual-writing for software installation, for example. According to Mr. Velasco, adults with autism should excel at jobs that require going step by step, without skipping details that other workers may miss.

The SAP program also includes training of managers in the benefits and challenges of autistic behaviors. "What we teach is clarity in communications, empathy, try to understand, put yourself in someone else's shoes. Most importantly, they need to be aware that this condition exists and it is in the best benefit of the company to employ people that bring this type of skill set."[63]

Joining SAP, the information technology firm, Computer Aid, Inc, announced in 2013 that it would aggressively seek out adults with autism for software tester positions. The company's goal, by the end of 2015, is that 3 percent of its workforce will be adults with autism.[64] Additionally, the mortgage lender Freddie Mac launched an autism employment effort, with a first full-time hire in January 2014. "Harnessing the unique skills of people on the autism spectrum has the potential to strengthen our business and make us more competitive," declared the Freddie Mac policy. Echoing SAP, the Freddie Mac spokesperson noted that "interns often perform well in testing and data modeling jobs that require great attention to detail . . . as a way of seeing things that might not have been anticipated by the developers."[65]

The most unusual targeted program for adults with autism has been a program started by the Israeli Army. According to ANSAmed, the Italian news agency, in February 2014, "the Israeli army has decided to continue enlisting autistic youths to take advantage of the extraordinary visual abilities some of them have to spot even the most imperceptible change in images. The young recruits are placed in Unit 9900: an elite, highly specialized corps of military intelligence. Its task is to study data and images transmitted by Israeli satellites orbiting the earth and provide detailed, sensitive information to field commanders."[66]

What We've Learned So Far About Autism and Technology Employment

Today's technology-employment initiatives are like most areas of autism employment: in a very early stage, with some placements and findings so far, but much more to be learned.

The stand-alone testing businesses have struggled financially. But their struggles have not been rooted in the difficulties of workers with autism to perform their software-testing responsibilities. Rather these businesses have struggled because of the inherent difficulties associated with the software-testing business: a great deal of competition, low profit margins, ongoing price undercutting, and new entrants into the field, including from offshore. As of this writing, ULTRA Testing of New York is in the best shape financially—though it has needed all of the expertise and contacts of its two high-powered entrepreneurs to remain competitive.

The main impact of these stand-alone testing businesses has been and may continue to be sparking interest in hiring adults with autism by the major software firms. Several major software employers, led by SAP, have launched autism-employment initiatives in the past year, focused on software tester positions. Though so far these initiatives have created only a few hundred jobs combined, they are spurring others in the technology industry to examine replication.

The results, at both stand-alone businesses and among major employers, suggest that at least some adults with autism have abilities and characteristics that make them good fits for these jobs, including concentration, great attention to detail, and tolerance for routine. There will never be enough software testing positions available to employ more than a small segment of adults with autism (and only a small segment of adults with autism will be interested in these jobs). But software testing and broader technology employment possibilities for adults with autism are not mirages. Even if they might have been overhyped, they should join and complement the other autism employment strategies set out in this book.

12

AUTISM AND THE INTERNET ECONOMY

AT A RECENT AASCEND board meeting, we were discussing the job club schedule when Adam Pollack, a senior member of our group in his sixties, interrupted: "I'm not looking for a job, I couldn't get a job, or hold a job. But I'd like to find some way of generating income."

He went on to say that he did "mathematical discoveries." Perhaps, he said, someone would pay him for these discoveries. Also, he had taken photographs over the years and "friends have suggested that they might be of value."

A number of our club members are in micro-businesses or other forms of self-employment, sometimes in addition to a part-time job. As set out in Chapter 6, Stacey has a pet-sitting business, Paul a handyman business, and Andrew does pillow design and sculpts in addition to his part-time recycling position. Additionally, we have Don who repairs computers and Craig who is a piano tuner.

Most of these market endeavors are marginal, bringing in a little income to supplement SSI or SSDI payments. At the same time, Adam's point about looking at economic participation and income beyond the concept of a job, is a sound one.

The Internet economy, and especially two parts of it, the share economy and the social mission economy, are reshaping the nature of employment. They are giving rise to more and more opportunities to generate income through efforts outside of traditional full-time or even part-time employment. These opportunities will be available to all persons, and may provide particular opportunities for the autism community.

The Internet Economy and the Share Economy

First, a word about the Internet economy, especially the Internet commerce/social media economy, and the employment opportunities it generates.

San Francisco is ground zero for this Internet commerce/social media economy in the United States and illustrates the economic activity being generated. Young entrepreneurs from around the world are flocking to the area, especially to a one-mile radius around Second and Howard streets in the South of Market district.

Walk through San Francisco's South of Market and nearby area and you find thousands of new business ventures. The entrepreneurs, usually in their twenties or early thirties, are engaged in businesses to provide goods and services in new ways through the Internet. The business offices may be a few desks or tables in a sparsely decorated room or two. Or they may be a series of laptops around a large table in a business incubator for newly established businesses or "business accelerator" for start-ups that have some track record. Rocketspace is one such business accelerator. It started in a former coffee warehouse at 181 Fremont and has recently moved to larger space a few blocks away, just above Market Street. As an accelerator it seeks to push forward technology start-ups, through flexible office space, sharing of ideas, access to capital, and access to technology talent.

Rocketspace houses around 120 start ups at any time. The line-up changes regularly since Rocketspace encourages companies to leave when they reach thirty employees. Among the start-ups operating recently in Rocketspace, indicating the range of products/services: ePantry, a company locating sustainable products; News360, a company aggregating and discovering Internet content via mobile devices; My Crowd, a company crowdsourcing one-off design tasks. A few Rocketspace alumni already have hit big: Uber, the car sharing company, and Leap Motion, the advanced motion sensor technology.

Beyond Rocketspace are six other tech accelerators in the area: HatchToday, the Hub, FoundersDen, WeWork, Runway, and the Hattery (with the tech training firm, General Assembly). Like Rocketspace, the other accelerators house a mix of Internet start-ups with various products/services, platforms for consumers to share information and crowdsourcing solutions.

HatchToday houses over eighty start-ups; a good number of them have strong social missions. EarthStarter is a startup dedicated to promoting urban gardening (producing an "all in one garden system that helps city dwellers grow food and flowers in small spaces"). HandsU is a mobile donation platform enabling persons to donate funds to specific homeless individuals they've met and to target these funds for specific services. Workhand aims to be a blue collar Linked-In, helping workers in the building trades to network and find projects and part-time work.

The nearby accelerator, the Hattery, is expressly focused on social mission start-ups. The Hattery management seeks out businesses with social goals. Among their current businesses are Puddle, developing "lending pools" for persons or businesses not able to obtain conventional financing; Art250, with the mission of linking artists to wider consumer markets; and Bright Funds, with a mission of identifying the most effective nonprofits for potential donors.

The new Internet economy/social media firms are creating direct employment not only for programmers and engineers, but also marketing specialists, account managers, and office-service workers. In San Francisco, during the three year period from 2010 to 2013, the city's technology/information cluster companies added 21,000 new jobs, reaching a total of 67,000 technology/information jobs by late 2013.[67]

Beyond the effect of direct employment is a far larger indirect employment impact, chiefly through a part of the Internet economy known as the share economy (or collaborative consumption economy). The share economy companies are Internet-based companies finding ways to utilize resources more effectively. These companies are creating ways that individuals outside of the business world can carve out part-time and sometimes full-time employment for themselves.

Airbnb is one of the share economy firms. Airbnb allows individuals to rent apartments and houses or singlerooms in a house to travelers as an alternative to hotels or other lodgings. Such rentals have been done on an informal, haphazard scale for many years. Airbnb routinized the process: expanding it and adding ways that hosts and travelers can do background checks, payment security, and insurance to cover damage or theft.

Airbnb's growth has generated jobs directly. Starting with the two founders working out of an apartment in 2007, the company grew to approximately 500 employees by late 2012 and over 600 by mid-2013—with plans to employ 1,000 people in a few years.

More broadly, Airbnb has created part-time employment for the hundreds of thousands of hosts across the world. These hosts have gained income in return for developing, arranging, and maintaining rentals.

Airbnb's success has helped generate other share economy start-ups that are enabling individuals to rent out unused residential rooms, as well as sites enabling individuals or businesses to rent out unused commercial spaces. Froomz, for example, is a start-up in the South of Market area created by Yan Heim. Heim received a degree in electrical engineering from Beijing University of Technology in 1991 and worked for twelve years in corporate finance at AT&T before joining the Internet economy. Froomz is building an Internet platform for owners of dance studios, offices, rooms in restaurants or other spaces to more fully utilize these spaces.

The share economy has spread to fuller utilization of goods beyond real estate: to cars, parking spaces, appliances, to name a few of these goods. Getaround enables individuals to rent their autos, and the even more specialized FlightCar enables individuals to rent autos they have parked at an airport. Parking Panda enables individuals to rent out driveways for parking at major events. SnapGoods enables individuals to rent out power drills, vacuum cleaners, or virtually any appliance.

Along with the sharing of goods, the share economy has come to include the sharing of labor and expertise. Vayable offers insider travel experiences, such as guided local food or history tours. It enables individuals to monetize their expertise as "guides" for, say, a tour of the best retail stores in San Francisco's Chinatown or a private sail on Monterey Bay or touring public art in the Mission District. TaskRabbit enables individuals to create or expand self-employment in delivery, house chores, shopping, and handyman tasks ("get just about anything done by safe, reliable, awesome people").

The share economy is in its early stages: businesses are starting-up and shutting down at a rapid pace. Yet, as a venture capitalist who has backed two car-sharing sites tells Forbes, "The share economy is a real trend . . . People really are looking at this for economic, environmental, and lifestyle reasons. By making this access as convenient as ownership, companies are seeing a major shift."[69]

The Internet Economy and the Social Mission Economy

Accompanying the share economy, the Internet economy is giving rise to a social mission economy. The social mission economy uses the tools of the Internet for addressing longstanding poverty, environmental, and employment challenges in new ways.

Several examples of social mission firms are noted above, connected to the business accelerators HatchToday and The Hattery. Additionally, there is a subset of social mission economy firms focused on job creation and employment, utilizing the powerful Internet tool of crowdfunding.

Prior to the 1980s, job creation strategies by state and local governments focused on larger companies, seen as the main generators of employment. The research of Professor David Birch and others in the 1980s helped shift economic development efforts to small businesses, including micro-businesses.[70] Based on this research, local/state governments and private foundations in the 1980s and 1990s established small business and micro-business loan funds and technical assistance tools targeted at high unemployment populations.

Today, the Internet economy is continuing the small business/micro-business focus for job generation and emphasis on high unemployment populations. But it is doing so in a far broader and more influential manner. The Internet tool of crowdfunding has brought new capital markets and energy to micro-business and small business development.

Through crowdfunding, tens or hundreds or even thousands of individuals are able to pool investments of $100, $50 or less, to fund businesses or individual projects and closely track and participate in the progress of these businesses or projects. The result has been hundreds of millions in loans and/or investments in businesses or projects, with the investments continuing to grow in number of lenders and amounts.

One of the chief Internet economy companies in this micro lending boom is Kiva. Headquartered in the South of Market area, on Howard near Fifth, Kiva started in 2005 with a focus on micro loans to entrepreneurs in developing countries. At its formation in 2005, few investors or others would have bet on a model of individuals investing in businesses that they've never seen and that in most cases are continents away.

Yet, the model turned out to be successful, far beyond expectations. By August 2013, Kiva had facilitated over 900,000 loans, totaling over $467 million in seventy-two countries. It had over 980,000 lenders throughout the world. In the Kiva model, the lender chooses a borrower based on information provided by Kiva field partners and volunteers. Though the loan is administered by an intermediary financial institution, the lender follows the loan repayment and progress of the business. As a loan is repaid, the lender is encouraged to plow back the loan repayment into another business.

In recent years, Kiva has increased its activity with micro-lending and small business lending in the United States. It has established a new product, KivaZip, which eliminates the intermediary institution and enables lenders to connect directly with borrowers. Initial loan amounts in KivaZip are modest, capped at $5,000, though once a borrower fully repays an initial loan, a further loan can be sought. Utilizing Internet tools, the lender can follow on a daily basis both the additional lenders coming on board as money is being raised and later the progress of repayment. Lenders are encouraged to be more than passive investors, to get to know the local business they invest in, and serve as ambassadors for these businesses.

Beyond Kiva and the other lending sites are the tens of major crowdsourcing sites that enable individuals to raise funds for specific projects (including Kickstarter, Indiegogo, RocketHub, and Fundly). Additionally, emerging sites such as Upstart and Pave enable individuals to raise funds in exchange for a percentage of their future income.

The Internet Economies and the Autism Community

What does the Internet economy and its share economy and social mission economy mean for the autism community and employment?

Three main connections stand out, which our Autism Job Club are pursuing.

First, is the ability of the micro-businesses started by our members to form business collectives for joint marketing, business strategy, administration. Though the business collective is possible without the Internet, the Internet allows micro-businesses to come together far more effectively than in the past and to target niche markets.

(Individuals in the autism community, along with their families, friends, and advocates, constitutes one such niche market.)

The club recently hosted a session featuring micro-business ventures by our members. Stacey talked about her pet-sitting business, Andrew about his pillow design, Craig about piano tuning. The session attracted not only our members but others in the Bay Area autism community who talked about their own micro-businesses: in jewelry design, in home repairs and handyman projects, in photography.

Discussion turned to how theses fragile micro-businesses might work together as autism community collectives. To date, we haven't found good examples of such autism collectives in the United States. But we are in contact with sf.citi, the industry association of Internet economy firms in San Francisco, to pursue this approach.

The second connection our job club is pursuing the ability of our members to tap into the employment opportunities that the share economy is creating. A few of our members own condos or their families own houses. They may want to rent out rooms or rent out other possessions. They might band together for administering and overseeing these efforts.

Elaine, in her forties, owns a family home in Walnut Creek. She once tried to rent out one or two of her rooms but was overwhelmed by the administrative details—insurance, advertising, choosing renters. Airbnb and the other sites make the process easier, especially if Elaine had someone with our club who could help her through it.

Further, our members may also be able to utilize some of their unusual, even savant, skills through the share economy. Adam, the job club member introduced at the start of this chapter, may not be able to market his mathematical discoveries. But he may be able to use his considerable math skills to tutor others or perhaps in some other way. Most of the savant skills of our members are not easily transferred into the market, such as William's ability to multiply large numbers in his head or tell what day of the week a date falls on ten years from now.

However, some skills may be applicable. The share economy opens up new possibilities.

The third connection is the crowdfunding approach of the social mission Internet economy. The hundreds of thousands of individual lenders on Kiva, Kickstarter, and Indiegogo, are not looking to maximize returns. Their motivations are influenced heavily by economic development for specific low-income communities or high-unemployment groups, such as at-risk youth, laid-off manufacturing workers, or adults with autism. Crowdfunding opens up a new set of funding possibilities for business ventures run by or employing people on the spectrum.

We often think of employment in terms of payroll jobs. This is by far the favored approach and goal of our most of our Autism Job Club members. But the Internet economy is expanding the domain of other self-employment or micro-business options. For our member Adam, these options may be primary answers. For others, they may be temporary options between jobs or options in addition to part-time jobs.

In both parts of the Internet economy, the share economy, and the social mission (crowdfunding) economy, the options are likely to be most effectively pursued through coming together as an autism community and functioning collectively as well as individually.

Part V
Autism and the Practical Economy

13

THE SURPRISING EMPLOYMENT GROWTH IN THE PRACTICAL ECONOMY

THE **EXPANSION** of the "knowledge economy" in the United States has been the focus of media attention. This is the economy of management consultants, computer systems analysts, financial analysts, medical and health services managers, and software developers.

However, far more jobs in the next decade will be in the non-knowledge or practical economy: jobs as retail clerks, bakers, health aides, customer service representatives, and office clerks.

Within the autism community, there is a wide range of talents and abilities. Some members will fit comfortably in the knowledge economy. But many may not. Fortunately, there will be many job options in the practical economy. Already, within the autism community there are efforts to target jobs in this practical economy, both through new business ventures and through employment with major employers.

The Knowledge Economy and Its Growth
Let's start with the knowledge economy and its job opportunities. Stanford University professors Walter Powell and Kaisa Snellman

define the knowledge economy as "production and services based on knowledge-intensive activities . . . The key component of a knowledge economy is a greater reliance on intellectual capabilities than on physical inputs or natural resources."[71] UC Berkeley professor Enrico Moretti links the knowledge economy employment to jobs that require college degrees or graduate degrees.[72] We will use the term knowledge economy jobs as shorthand for jobs that typically (though not always) require at least bachelor degrees and/or substantial analytic and creative skills.

Figure 13-1 presents the U.S. Bureau of Labor Statistics (BLS) occupational projections for the period 2012–2022, targeting the top twenty of occupations that require at least a bachelor's degree. As can be seen, a variety of occupations within the knowledge economy are projected to be expanding significantly in the near future. Some, but not all, are linked to technology. Computer systems analysts, software developers, network and computer systems administrators make the list, but also teachers, financial analysts, medical and health service managers, management consultants—all led by general and operations managers.

Today, the knowledge economy receives a lot of attention in both the academic and popular presses. A number of prominent economists have been trumpeting it as the main driver of future American prosperity and job creation. "The Human Capital Century" is the title that Professor Moretti gives the concluding chapter of his 2012 book, *The New Geography of Jobs*. He argues that America and each individual city faces a challenge between being part of this knowledge economy or being left behind. Moretti declares, "The number and strength of a country's brain hubs will determine whether it will prosper or decline. Physical factories will keep losing importance, but cities with a larger percentage of interconnected, highly educated workers will become the new factories where ideas and knowledge are forged."

Similarly, Harvard professors Lawrence Katz and Claudia Goldin are emphatic about the knowledge economy's role as employment driver, in their magisterial *The Race Between Education and Technology*.[73] Katz and Goldin analyze wage data and educational attainment over the past two centuries in the United States. Up through the 1970s, they argue, education gains outpaced technology. Since the 1970s, though, technology has outpaced education, meaning a shortage of knowledge economy workers.

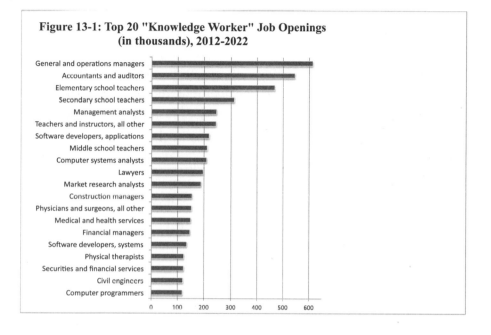

Figure 13-1: Top 20 "Knowledge Worker" Job Openings (in thousands), 2012-2022

According to Katz and Goldin, the number of jobs in the knowledge economy that were created by technology have been outpacing the college-educated workforce needed to fill these jobs. Training workers for the knowledge economy results in both a reduction in unemployment and a reduction in wage differentials.

Proponents such as Katz and Golden rightly bring to our attention opportunities in this economy. However, they often overstate the knowledge economy's effects on employment. Bureau of Labor Statistics data and projections show greater job growth outside of the knowledge economy, in what might be termed the practical economy. This is clear from the following series of charts drawing on BLS data.

The Even Larger Growth of the Non-Knowledge or Practical Economy

Figure 13-2 shows the fifteen occupations with most the job openings between 2012 and 2022 as projected by the BLS. Only one, registered nurse, requires a postsecondary degree. The others require only a high-school diploma. The occupations with the most openings include retail salespersons, food preparation and service, cashiers, office clerks, waitstaff, customer service representatives, laborers, and other support occupations.

The job openings measured in Figure 13-2 combine both jobs to be added (growth) and replacement due to turnover. Since jobs requiring less formal education generally have higher turnover than other jobs, the list skews toward jobs in the practical economy. However, looking only at job growth, the practical-economy jobs still dominate. Of the top ten occupations in projected job growth, only one, registered nurses (#2) requires formal college education. The list of occupations with greatest job growth is filled out with personal care aides (#1), retail salespersons (#3), home health aides (#4), combined food preparation and serving workers (#5), nursing assistants (#6), secretaries and administrative assistants (#7), customer service repre-sentatives (#8), janitors and cleaners (#9), and laborers (#10).

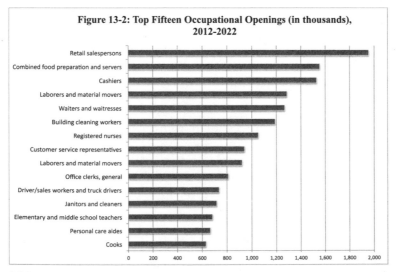

Figure 13-2: Top Fifteen Occupational Openings (in thousands), 2012-2022

A diverse economy requires diverse individuals fulfilling a wide range of necessary activities in a modern world. Microchips, cellular technology, software, and the Internet have not supplanted the need for grocers, cooks, dry cleaners, gardeners, or health care workers. Even in our postindustrial economy most jobs do not require a college education.

Figure 13-3 shows the dominance of the practical economy in another form. It displays job openings by the education levels required. Between 2012 and 2022 there is job growth in all segments of the pyramid, but by far the most in jobs requiring a high school education or less.

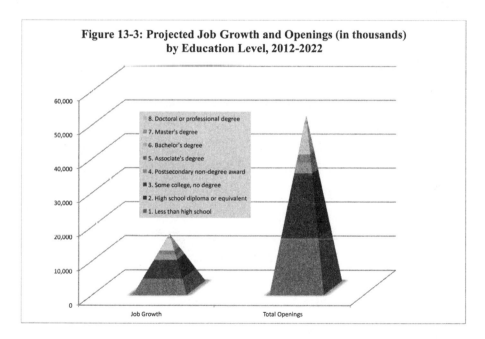

Figure 13-3: Projected Job Growth and Openings (in thousands) by Education Level, 2012-2022

8. Doctoral or professional degree
7. Master's degree
6. Bachelor's degree
5. Associate's degree
4. Postsecondary non-degree award
3. Some college, no degree
2. High school diploma or equivalent
1. Less than high school

Proponents of the knowledge economy frequently assert that jobs requiring a bachelor's degree or above are projected to grow at rates above the growth rates of other jobs. As shown in Figure 13-4, this is true. However, their percentage of total job growth remains small, since they start as a small minority of jobs. More than 60 percent of projected job growth is in jobs that require high school degrees or less.

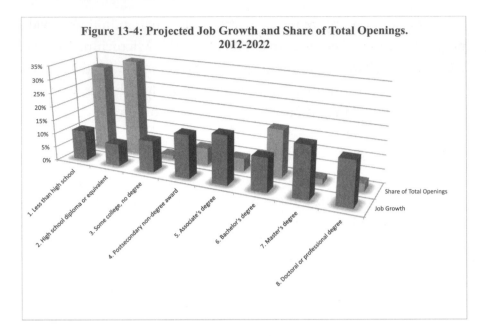

Figure 13-4: Projected Job Growth and Share of Total Openings. 2012-2022

Wide Diversity of Jobs in the Practical Economy

What does the growth within the practical economy mean for job placement strategies? First, practical-economy employment spans a wide range of sectors and occupations. The frequent articles on the "hot" jobs in the American economy usually give a highly distorted view of the job market. These articles make it seem as if we will all be in the information sector as software engineers, programmers, or website designers, or in the health-care sector, as nurses, health counselors, or other types of health-care workers.

Yet, as shown in Figure 13-5, the future will continue to see a need for workers in sixteen or seventeen different sectors. These sectors include "old economy" sectors such as manufacturing and transportation/warehousing, as well as sectors usually associated with the "new economy," including professional and business services, educational services, and information technology.

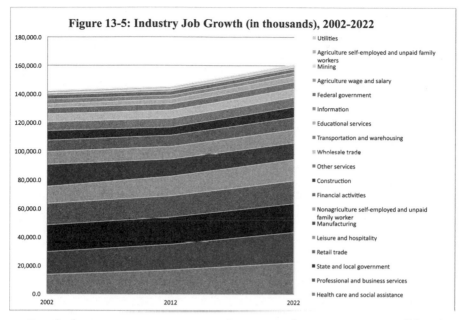

Figure 13-5: Industry Job Growth (in thousands), 2002-2022

Similarly, among occupations, diversity of opportunities will be the hallmark of the emerging practical economy. Figure 13-5 sets out the industries within the practical economy that for which there are the greatest number of openings and also the greatest growth. Beyond these industries are hundreds of others that will need workers: bakers, landscaping and grounds keeping workers, warehouse workers, and automobile mechanics.

In the next chapters we turn to how this practical economy job growth can accommodate the wide range of abilities among adults with autism—especially the segment of adults without post-secondary education.

14

AUTISM-FOCUSED BUSINESSES AND HIRING INITIATIVES IN THE PRACTICAL ECONOMY

IN RECENT YEARS, a number of autism employment initiatives have targeted jobs in the practical economy. Some of these initiatives have involved businesses in the practical economy, such as car washes, candle-making shops, bakeries, and food trucks focused on hiring adults with autism. Others have involved major employers in the practical economy, Walgreens and Best Buy, increasing their hiring of adults with autism.

Autism Focused Businesses in the Practical Economy

One of the best-known of the autism-focused businesses has been the Rising Tide Car Wash, located in Parkland, Florida, which employs adults with autism.

Rising Tide was formally launched in April 2013 by John D'Eri, whose son Andrew is an adult with autism. Within a year, the car wash employed thirty-five adults and was celebrated in the national media as a model for autism employment in the practical economy. In 2014, John D'Eri was featured on the *NBC Nightly News* and invited to speak at the TED conference in Miami.

In his TED talk, Mr. D'Eri described the worry about his son's future that drove him and other family members to start the car wash—even though they had no experience in the field. "What will my family member with autism do when I am no longer around to take care of him? If you're like us, this question has not only crossed your mind but keeps you up at night.

"When I thought of Andrew, I could not see an independent man at age forty. Instead, I could only see him living at home, with no sense of purpose, no friends, no social ties."

D'Eri, with another son, Thomas, started to think of a car wash as early as 2011. They researched similar businesses and traveled the country to learn of other autism-employment efforts. In spring 2013, they hired their first workers, including Andrew, and gradually have brought on other workers.

Of his son Andrew, John D'Eri explained that "Although a vibrant, lighthearted young man, Andrew's disability is a clear competitive disadvantage when it comes to securing gainful employment. We believe that Andrew and others like him have difficulty getting a job, not because they don't have the tools to be top-notch employees, but rather because most businesses are simply not structured in a way that allows them to reach their full potential."

The car wash enables Andrew and his coworkers to interact with customers in a way that they cannot do in most other business environments. This is valuable for the workers and also valuable in spreading the word about the job abilities of adults with autism.

In John's view, his business has a competitive advantage because of the strengths of his workforce. He claims his workers are more detail-oriented than other car-wash workers. They also are more loyal and grateful to have the job opportunity.

After one year, John already is talking about expanding Rising Tide and expanding into other autism-focused businesses in the practical economy. He has formed CanDo Business Ventures in order to franchise Rising Tide to other families with autism. He envisions getting into other business lines that deploy "scalable, consumer-facing businesses that are centered around providing employment for people with autism."

Rising Tide is among the best-known of the autism-focused businesses, but by no means the only one. Autism-focused businesses, based in the practical economy, are being launched on a regular basis. A good number are in agricultural or gardening pursuits. Among those that are most advanced are Roses for Autism in Connecticut, a rose-growing business,[74] the TIAA-CREF apple orchards in central Washington, and the businesses that make up the Agricultural Communities for Adults with Autism. Agricultural Communities is a consortium of more than thirty businesses that provide employment for adults with autism in agricultural enterprises (Lettuce Work in Ohio that employs adults with autism in growing and distribution of organically grown lettuce, Erik's Ranch in Minnesota that offers employment in gardening and equestrian grooming).[75] In almost all cases, these businesses, like the Rising Tide Car Wash, have been started by parents frustrated with the lack of mainstream employment opportunities for their children.[76]

Other autism-focused businesses have been in service and retail pursuits. Extraordinary Ventures of Chapel Hill has launched businesses to employ adults with autism in laundry services, premium candles, and office services. A special-education teacher has been the driving force behind The Mini Man Monkey Brains candy store in downtown Skokie, Illinois, which employs adults with autism and other neurological differences. The ARC of Schenectady, New York, has partnered with a local entrepreneur to start Puzzles Bakery and Café. The Puzzles entrepreneur told the local radio station, "People with autism make really good employees. They're very willing and happy to be here."

Rising Tide and the other autism-focused businesses follow in a line of business ventures, known as social-enterprise businesses, as they have goals beyond profitability. Usually their main goal is providing employment or transitional employment for high unemployment groups. Social-enterprise businesses have been developed to employ ex-offenders, at-risk youth, and ex-addicts, as well as adults with disabilities.

The record of social enterprise businesses in the United States is a mixed one. Over the past three decades, hundreds of social-enterprise businesses have been launched in the areas noted above, as well as in landscaping, baked goods, carpet cleaning, and janitorial services.[77] There have been economic struggles. In the majority of cases these social-enterprise businesses have required subsidies, sometimes very generous subsidies, to stay in the market place. They may cease operations when subsidies end or when the entrepreneurial founders move on.

Despite this mixed economic record of social enterprises, the social-enterprise movement is very much alive today, in the autism community and beyond. One of the main thought leaders in the social-enterprise movement today is the group, REDF founded in 1997 by financier George R. Roberts of the private equity investment firm KKR & Co. Roberts's vision is of a network of social-enterprise businesses throughout California and he has donated millions of dollars to push forward this vision. These businesses provide transitional employment for high-unemployment groups in a more cost-effective manner than traditional government programs.

REDF's current portfolio consists of ten to twelve social enterprises that it helps fund in the practical economy: for example, a landscaping services and mattress recycling business targeting ex-addicts in San Jose, a pest management business in Los Angeles to hire the homeless, a maintenance and janitorial service in San Diego hiring ex-offenders. The REDF executive director, Carla Javits, and her staff oversee these businesses. They are proponents of the businesses' value in employing targeted groups. But they also are honest on the amount of time and funding needed to keep each business going and the fragile nature of most of these businesses.[78]

Autism Focused Hiring Initiatives by Major Employers in the Practical Economy

Constituting a greater scale of employment in the practical economy, several nationwide retailers have established employment initiatives for adults with autism. Among these have beeng Walgreens, Safeway, and Best Buy. Walgreens' autism initiative is the most far-reaching.

Walgreens first focused on hiring adults with autism as warehouse workers at a distribution center in Anderson, South Carolina, in 2007. In staffing this warehouse, Walgreens did not recruit exclusively adults with autism, but made such hiring a priority. In 2011, four years after the distribution center opened, Walgreens' Manager of Outreach and Employee Services, Deb Russell, noted that while she could not say how many adults with autism worked at Anderson, nearly 40 percent of the 550 to 600 Anderson employees identified as an adult with a disability. "Autism is a model disability for us," Ms. Russell told Professor Scott Standifer of the University of Missouri.[79]

Russell meant that Walgreens had developed a "toolbox" for recruitment and retention for autism that it subsequently applied to other disabilities. The four main toolbox elements were described by Walgreens as follows:

- Resources on disability etiquette
- Customized lessons for managers and supervisors on the features of different disabilities
- Job aids for common tasks in the facilities
- A social skills training curriculum for new hires with autism and related disorders, if needed

These elements might be more simply summarized as patience, flexibility, available job coaches, and educating managers and other workers about certain common characteristics of autism.

By 2011, Walgreens had expanded its autism hiring initiative to other distribution centers, including its one-million square-foot Walgreens Distribution Center in Windsor, Connecticut—where 35 percent to 40 percent of the 500 employees identified as having a disability. The company commissioned a study by several safety professionals, inside and outside of Walgreens, on the safety and performance results at the centers.

The study was published in June 2012 in the journal, *Professional Safety*.[80] Titled "Creating an Inclusive Workplace: Integrating Employees with Disabilities Into a Distribution Center Environment," it claimed that on measures of productivity and employee turnover, the workers with disabilities at the centers outperformed other workers. Regarding productivity, thirty-one distinct work stations were analyzed at three centers, including the Anderson center. In eighteen locations, the difference in productivity rates was statistically insignificant, in three locations, the employees without a disability were more productive, and in ten locations, employees with a disability were rated more productive.

Regarding employee turnover, the employees with disabilities had significantly lower turnover rates. Turnover for a three-year period was 48 percent lower among workers with disabilities than among the general worker population.

The authors note that Walgreens started with three center jobs identified as potential good fits for workers with disabilities due to the straightforward nature of tasks. The company created an on-site training room to simulate the work environment of these jobs, with tasks, summarized by the authors, as follows:

> *Case check in:* The employee removes a box of product from a pallet and verifies it against a purchase order. S/he then uses a scanner to enter its UPC into the inventory management system.

> *De-trash:* The employee removes a box of product from a conveyor, opens its outer carton and discards all bulk packaging before placing the product into a tote for storage.

> *Split-case pick:* This job involves manual picking of orders of partial cases of product, then placing picked items into a tote on a conveyor in preparation for shipping to the requested store.

These jobs have remained a focus of placement, but other distribution jobs have been added such as lift truck operator, computer room operator, and utility maintenance.

The authors single out three strategies utilized by Walgreens that they see as leading to program effectiveness.

- Creating partnerships with state and local social services agencies early in the process to assist with initial screening and training of candidates on an ongoing basis.
- Building a physical workplace conducive to accommodating employees with different abilities. Focus on building design, equipment selection, and management practices to maximize efficiency among workers of all abilities.
- Creating a welcoming and accepting culture in the building from the first day of operations.

The prime mover of the Walgreens initiative was Randy Lewis, the senior vice president of supply chain and logistics at Walgreens, who in 2007 had an eighteen-year-old son with autism. He would later write in 2012 about his motivation and outlook, in a post worth quoting at length:

> Ever since my son was diagnosed with autism in 1995, I've worried about him. How will he spend his days after aging out of the school system. Will any company ever hire him? Ironically, I began heading up the supply chain and logistics division around the same time as the diagnosis. I wanted to become a more inclusive employer but was timid because I didn't want to seem to be putting my personal life ahead of my professional responsibilities.

> Gradually it dawned on me that personal passion and business success can coexist. When it came time to build a new state-of-the-art distribution center in Anderson, SC, my presentation to the Walgreens board was relatively simple: Our new DC will be our most expensive and it will provide the best return we've ever had on any capital investment. And by the way, we hope to create an integrated work environment and staff so that one third of the

employees will be people with disabilities. Same standards, same pay, side by side.

When board members asked what would happen if business were adversely affected, I assured them we would adjust the percentage of employees with a disability until we met our performance goals. The Anderson DC opened in 2007, so we're coming up on five years of operational and safety data. The results have been all that I hoped they would be. In comparing the worker population with disabilities to the one without, the workers with disabilities have amassed records that show greater retention, productivity, and equal safety.[81]

Beyond Walgreens, other major retailers, including Safeway and Best Buy, have launched autism-focused hiring initiatives in the past few years. These have been based on principles similar to the Walgreens autism initiative: inclusion with the regular workforce, partnering with social services agencies specializing in autism, identifying positions that might be good fits.[82]

James Emmett, a rehabilitation counselor by trade, was a consultant to Walgreens; he implemented the Anderson Distribution Center from 2004 through 2006. He then helped Best Buy establish its own distribution center, emphasizing inclusion of workers with autism and other neurodiverse conditions. Mr. Emmett estimates that of the 75–80 employees working at any time in recent years at the Best Buy center, a quarter to a third were workers with autism or other neurodiverse conditions.

The Best Buy distribution center is located near Louisville, Kentucky, in Shepardsville. The employment inclusion initiative, like the initiative at Walgreens, was driven from the top down, from its corporate headquarters in Richfield, Minnesota. Best Buy executives had learned of the Anderson distribution center, toured the facility, and set out to replicate its inclusion model. The company partnered with a local agency, Options Unlimited, for recruitment, selection, and on-going counsel with managers and employees. For outreach, it organized a "Best Buy Coalition," comprised of the public and private agencies in the region serving workers with disabilities. "The Coalition and Options Unlimited have been a tremendous resource," the center's director Pam Smyth commented, "They are a large part of our success."

Mr. Emmett notes that like the Walgreens distribution center, the Best Buy center was equipped with physical modifications to encourage inclusion: dampening of sounds, sight lines, and equipment selection. But, as with Walgreens, more important than the physical adaptations was adapting the conditions of work culture, with an emphasis on: patience, flexibility, acceptance of certain personal quirks and rigidities, allowing job coaches, and sending a clear message of corporate buy-in. As Mr. Emmett explains, "The management team's flexibility and openness while maintaining high expectations created a culture that made the Best Buy distribution center in Kentucky one of the most disability-inclusive workplaces in the country."

***

One theme running through both the autism-focused businesses in the practical economy and the hiring initiatives is the competitive advantages that adults with autism often have in the ares of attention to detail, care, and craft. In the next chapter, let us elaborate on these values, especially the values of craft.

15

AUTISM, CRAFT, AND CALLING

ADULTS WITH AUTISM often will bring a craft to their jobs that makes them better workers in many situations. This is true throughout the economy, but especially in the practical economy.

The concept of craft encompasses several values: a care for detail, a willingness to invest time in a task to get it right, a commitment to quality beyond any monetary reward. "Calling" is a related concept—finding meaning and pleasure in the work itself, going beyond the effort required or expected.

Craft and calling are not new concepts. But they are finding new relevance in the American economy, particularly in the practical economy. Autism's competitive advantage is bolstered as America rediscovers craft.

The Reemergence of Craft in the Practical Economy

Let's begin with the rediscovery of craft, in the unlikely venue of television.

In the early 2000s, it would have been difficult to find anyone in the entertainment industry predicting the popularity of "work reality" television shows about bakers, car repair persons, and hairstylists. Yet, these shows appeared in the next few years, found an audience in the general public, and brought fresh insights about work. Work reality shows such as *Cake Boss*, *America's Next Top Model*, *American Pickers*, *Pawn Stars*, and *Tabitha's Salon Takeover* not only achieved ratings, but also generated numerous related shows in their occupations.

The success of these shows is in how the profiled workers perform their jobs. Jobs termed "throwaway" by policy commentators a few years earlier are shown as sources of dignity and satisfaction to these workers.

Throughout the 1990s and early 2000s, policy analysis and journalism often portrayed employment in the practical economy as something to be avoided at all costs. No matter that these jobs usually provided a service that people desired (car repair, haircare, nursing home care, for example) or produced a real product (baked goods, pawn shop items). Still, they were often characterized as disposable, distinguished by lack of challenge, tedium, low status, and low wages.

Barbara Ehrenreich's *Nickel and Dimed: On (Not) Getting By in America*, published in 2001, was instrumental in shaping this view.[83] As part of her research, Ehrenreich had taken a series of low-wage service jobs over a year's period—as a waitress in Florida, a housecleaner and nursing home aide in Maine, and a Walmart employee in Minnesota. She applied for these jobs without indicating her education or background. She lived only on the wages she earned, which meant she stayed in cheap motels and apartments.

Ehrenreich is a talented observer and writer, and her book largely shaped the perception of jobs in the practical economy. As described in *Nickle and Dimed*, these jobs are distinguished by their low wages, well below what is needed to support a family. These jobs have no opportunities for mobility. Further, they are characterized by difficult physical labor (waitressing, cleaning hotel rooms, nursing home care), unsafe and unsanitary conditions, and/or constant petty humiliations (psychological tests and drug tests).

Also in 2001, Ben Cheever published *Selling Ben Cheever: Back to Square One in a Service Economy*, his memoir of working in entry-level service jobs. It amounted to a critique of the non-knowledge job world.[84] Like Ehrenreich, Cheever is a college graduate, though unlike Ehrenreich he did not hide his background, even as he took service sector jobs outside the knowledge economy. Over a period of five years he worked as a Burns security guard, a telemarketer, a salesman at CompUSA, a salesman at Nobody Beats the Wiz, a sandwich maker at Cosi Sandwich Bar, and a car salesman at Wegman Auto.

Downsizing is a main theme of the book and Cheever introduces the reader to several former while-collar workers he meets in these jobs who have been fired or downsized from higher-status and higher paying jobs: a former IBM manager who is working at the car lot on commission, a certified public accountant who is working at the computer store, a Burns security guard who tells Cheever he'd been a phone company executive. Other themes are the tedium, repetition, and difficulty of surviving on the low wages of sandwich making or as a security guard or a commission salesperson.

Even at the time of these books and other critiques of the service sectors, a number of writers dissented from the conventional wisdom. They showed the practical economy jobs in some positive light, including the craft possible in the jobs. A few followed the approach of Ehrenreich and Cheever and took practical economy jobs. Charles Platt, a senior editor at *Wired Magazine*, took a job at Walmart, and though he highlighted the low pay, he also highlighted the craft possible in a retail clerk position.[85] Adam Shepard, a recent college graduate, set out with $25 in his pocket in Charleston, South Carolina, living in a homeless shelter. He moved through a series of practical economy positions to show the income and mobility possible even in low wage jobs.[86]

The reemergence of craft in the practical economy, though, found its fullest expression in the first decade of the 2000s with the rise of the work reality shows. These shows focused not on the knowledge economy jobs of analysts, lawyers, accountants, software engineers, web designers. Instead, they showed craft and meaning in the jobs of bakers, car repair persons, waiters, ice road truckers, pawn store owners, and antique restorers. It's worth describing four of the highest rated of these shows, since they celebrated diverse forums for craft.

The Cake Boss premiered on April 19, 2009, on the TLC network. The main character is Buddy Valastro, who runs a bakery in Hoboken, New Jersey. The bakery, Carlo's Bake Shop, has a baking and sales crew of nearly thirty, including Buddy's mother, four sisters, and three brothers-in-law.

On the surface, the *Cake Boss* episodes are standard sitcom fare. On Christmas Eve, the crew must pull together to meet a rush of customers, which allows Buddy to reflect on the importance of family. A drag queen, Miss Richfield 1981, orders a "happy holidays" pop-up cake, which the crew must deliver to her New York City show. The shop's two delivery guys, Anthony and Stretch, dress up as elves to deliver a cake to a women's fashion business.

What is original, compelling, and important about the show is the job values it demonstrates. Buddy and his crew do not approach baking as low skilled, production work. Instead, they are craftsmen; operating with creativity, care for detail, and willingness to put in time to get the product just right. Buddy and crew approach the pop-up cake and the women's fashion cake as works of art, just as they approach the other theme cakes they create (robot cake, roller stake cake, billiards table cake, and life-size race car cake). "I'll redo a cake ten times if I have to," Buddy says of his drive. "I'll work, you know, four days straight. I will do what I have to do to get the job done." Even with the non-theme items, the regular cupcakes, cookies, and pies, Buddy and crew continually are looking for ways to innovate, improve, be creative.

Though Buddy calculates how to make money, he also approaches the bakery as a calling. Through the bakery, he is serving others. He is providing his customers, mainly Hoboken residents, with quality cakes and cookies that they value and derive pleasure from. Further, through his response to customer demand, he creates a job not only for himself but also employment for others.

Cake Boss followed other shows featuring the craft of bakery workers, *Ace of Cakes* and *Amazing Wedding Cakes*, as well as the craft of cupcake specialists, *The Cupcake Wars*, *The Cupcake Girls*, and *DC Cupcakes.* "

America's Next Top Model (ANTM) premiered in May 2003, on the UPN network, and quickly became one of the highest rated shows on the network, continuing for over twenty seasons (two seasons per year). Despite on-going changes in the judging panel, the format remained similar: each season started with ten to fourteen contestants and in each episode one contestant was eliminated, based on modeling ability.

ANTM was criticized for over-emphasizing female physical appearance. Yet, the main message of *ANTM* was exactly the opposite. Listen each week to host Tyra Banks and technical advisors Jay Manuel and J. Alexander: modeling is far more than looking good, modeling is a craft. A model cannot simply show up. She must study the rules and norms of modeling, must understand photo-shoot directions, must master the runway walk. J. Alexander, the runway adviser, speaks about balance and posture and meeting the client's goals, rarely about looks.

American Pickers premiered on the History Channel in January 2010 and has continued to the present. It focuses on Mike Wolfe and Frank Fritz whose business is "picking," traveling throughout the country to purchase antiques and collectibles from ordinary people. Usually, the goods are in run-down condition and are in need of repair or restoration. The pickers try to identify the gems among the bars and attics of junk.

For Mike and Frank, their business is craft and calling. They are looking to make a profit in their antique restorations—each week, the pickers announce, "We'll buy anything we can make money on" and "Where other people see junk, we see dollar signs." In practice, though, they purchase antiques that will not be profitable, but are objects of beauty or importance that should not be lost. Mike purchases a rusting guitar which he'll probably lose money on because he believes it should be rescued; so too with Mike's collection of Indian motorcycles and vintage bicycles that are more labors of love than money makers.

Pawn Stars is another work reality show on the History channel, premiering in July 2009 and continuing to the present. It focuses on the workers at the world famous Gold & Silver Pawn Shop, a family-owned pawn shop in Las Vegas, Nevada. The main character is Rick Harrison, and he works with his father Richard "Old Man" Harrison, son Corey "Big Hoss" Harrison, and Corey's friend Austin "Chumlee" Russell.

These pawn shop workers daily meet with customers who bring in a wide range of items, from old cars to silver goods and furniture, to sell or pawn. The workers provide history lessons on the items, as well as discussion of their cost estimates. The pawn shop becomes not a cheap and empty means of commerce. Rather, it is an on-going history lesson by workers whose mission is to identify and rescue artifact.

Beyond these four shows are more than twenty work-reality spin-offs, variations and competitors in the same industries and others: *Pimp My Ride* on workers in an auto custom repair shop, *Tabitha's Salon Takeover* and *Shear Genius* on hairstylists, *Ice Road Truckers* on long-haul truck drivers in isolated areas of Canada.

Craft, Calling, and the Autism Workforce

How refreshing are these work reality shows! How much can they help all workers, those with autism and the neurotypicals, recapture jobs in the practical economy? These shows push back against the idea of "throwaway" jobs and help inject both quality and meaning in work tasks.

This point about meaning is worth elaborating. The same job that one baker, hairstylist, or nursing home attendant might regard as without meaning, can be a source of pride for another worker. It all depends on perspective and craft.

Perhaps no book expresses the values of perspective and craft in the practical economy better than one of the early 1970s, Studs Terkel's

Working.[87] Terkel's book, subtitled, *People Talk About What They Do All Day and How They Feel About What They Do*, is an oral history of workers primarily in practical economy jobs: waitress, bookbinder, cement mason, gravedigger, and other "non-knowledge" occupations. The popularity of the book was due in good part to the craft described in these jobs and how workers injected meaning in their work.

A waitress tells Terkel, "When I put the plate down, you don't hear a sound. When I pick up a glass, I want it to be just right. When someone says, 'How come you're just a waitress?' I say, 'Don't you think you deserve being served by me?'"

A bookbinder takes pleasure in repairing old books because "a book is a life." A gravedigger takes pride in the neat lines and square edges of his work.

In the years since *Working* was published, other books have addressed this relation of craft and work meaning in our post-industrial economy, notably Robert Schrank's *Ten Thousand Working Days*[88] and Don Snyder's *The Cliff Walk*. In *The Cliff Walk: A Job Lost and a Life Found*, Don Snyder, a former college professor, details his loss of job in academia and reemergence as a carpenter.[89] Snyder first describes how he loses his job as a college English professor, remains unemployed for a lengthy period of time, and is reduced to supporting his family through food stamps and handouts. He slowly gets his life back together, first by taking a job as a golf course maintenance man ($8 an hour), then as a carpenter ($15 an hour), and finally as a handyman ($18 an hour). As the book ends, he is getting back to a middle-class lifestyle. Much of the book is about the satisfaction and craft Snyder finds as carpenter and handyman, in providing a service that his client homeowners need.

For adults with autism, craft will offer a source of meaning. It will also offer a competitive advantage in many cases. The founders of the autism-focused businesses and autism-focused hiring initiatives of the previous chapter see their experiences as bearing out a competitive advantage in craft. Other professionals in autism employment have come to this conclusion.

In Chapter 11, on technology employment, technology professionals spoke of the autism advantage in certain technology positions, such as software testing and quality control. These professionals identified abilities in concentration, comfort with repetition, and memory for detail that were held by many adults with autism and central to job performance.

So, too, these abilities are main elements of performance and craft in the practical economy, and linked to adults with autism. For car wash owner John D'Eri, his workers with autism perform better than other car wash workers in the areas of concentration, attention to detail, and loyalty. Heather Davis, the parent of a son with autism and prime mover behind the TIAA-CREFF apple orchards business, claims that the ten apple harvesters with autism perform better through their concentration and routine than other harvesters. "Most people not on the autism spectrum get bored," Davis told an interviewer, but for someone with autism "routine isn't such a problem for them."[90] The performance study of the workers with autism at the Walgreens distribution centers reported better performance outcomes by these workers and lower turnover.

Going forward, an autism advantage in the skills linked to craft needs to be further explored, documented, and built upon. Job coaches and counselors and others who work with adults with autism, including family members, need to be aware of the advantage, help cultivate these craft skills, and sell these skills to employers.

By no means will all workers with autism possess these craft skills, but experience so far should give us hope that many will do so. Approaching employers under the banner of craft will be the better strategy for expanding autism's domain in the practical economy.

16

AUTISM AND THE MOVEMENT TO IMPROVE WAGES IN THE PRACTICAL ECONOMY

RECENTLY, CINDY ZOELLER, a job club facilitator, emailed that one of our members, Max, had obtained a job at Safeway as a bagger. We all were pleased to see this and the announcement generated several congratulatory emails. It's so difficult to get any job today. Moreover, Safeway is a stable organization and if Max can do well, he should have at least some form of the job security that our members are seeking.

At the same time, several other former job club members who work at Safeway and other major groceries are only employed part-time (fewer than thirty hours). Or they work in smaller, non-union retail stores, part-time and at lower wages. They do not earn enough to live independently. Like other AASCEND members in lower wage practical economy jobs, they rely on other family resources or, increasingly, on SSI/SSDI disability insurance—as set out in Chapter 4.

Low wages and part-time employment in many practical economy jobs are concerns that extend far beyond the autism community. But they also increasingly are autism community concerns—as the goals of independent living and not being dependent on government benefits become more widespread. Influencing wage levels and work hours, though, have been elusive targets for the community—as for the wider society.

The Greater Skills Required in Practical Economy Jobs—But Persistent Differentials in Wages

In Chapter 13, we distinguished between jobs in the knowledge economy and practical economy. But the differences between the two types of jobs are declining. The need for technological and analytic skills have worked their way into the practical economy.

As automobiles have become more sophisticated technologically, mechanics now must understand the sensors and computer chips that control the engine and other automotive features. Heating, ventilation, and air conditioning technicians must now master the chemical refrigerants, computer-controlled systems, conventional and modern heat pumps, solar panels, and economizers. Machinists now employ precision computer-controlled devices that can machine parts with razor-thin precision.

However, at the same time that jobs in the practical economy are requiring greater knowledge skills, the wage differential between knowledge and practical economy jobs is not declining.[91] Figures 16-1 and 16-2 show the average occupational wages of occupational groups and the inflation-adjusted wage changes between 2002 and 2012. All of these occupational groups have seen wage gains in this period, but the larger gains have been concentrated among the knowledge economy jobs, and not the practical economy jobs.

To illustrate, we might start with the manufacturing sector. In manufacturing, computer-driven machinery is the new generation of manufacturing equipment. This computer-driven manufacturing, also known as "advanced manufacturing," requires manufacturing workers to now master computer operation skills. The advanced manufacturing worker is aptly described by a community college instructor as "a hybrid of an old-school machinist and a computer programmer."[92]

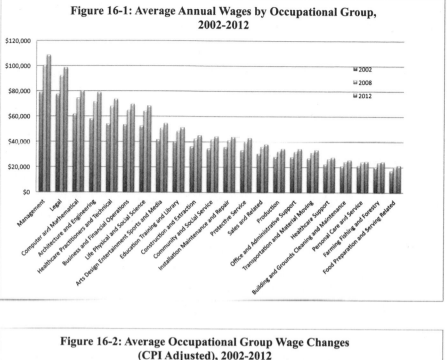

Figure 16-1: Average Annual Wages by Occupational Group, 2002-2012

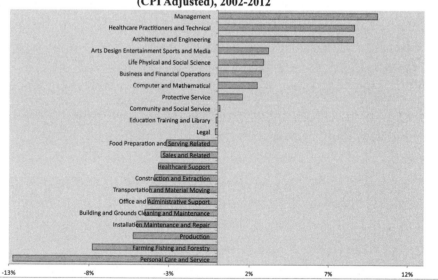

Figure 16-2: Average Occupational Group Wage Changes (CPI Adjusted), 2002-2012

Queensborough Community College in New York offers a training program in advanced manufacturing. The curriculum brings together courses in metallurgy, physics, and computer coding. The students learn not only to cut metal but also to write code telling a machine how to cut metal.[93]

The new skills required of the advanced manufacturing workers, though, are not reflected in increased wages. Advanced manufacturing jobs generally start at $10–$15 an hour for a worker with an AA degree, going up to $18 an hour after a few years. A nationwide study by the Boston Consulting Group found that wages in manufacturing were not keeping up with the technical skills that are increasingly required and that workers with advanced manufacturing skills were going into other occupations.[94]

The combination of increased need for technical skills and limited wage gains characterizes other expanding occupations in the practical economy, including certified nursing assistants in long-term care facilities, home health/personal care aides, and warehouse/logistics workers.

Certified nursing assistants (CNAs) provide the direct patient care in long-term care facilities. Training for CNA certification is six months. According to Ken Merchant, the former education director at the California Association of Health Facilities, CNAs now need to be tech-literate in operating the electronic medical records systems and electronic collection of personal information. Additionally, greater technical medical knowledge is required in order to care for patients with dementia, diabetes, and other ailments.

Despite the need for more sophisticated skills, including tech skills, the wages for CNAs have not increased significantly during the past decade in California. These wages range from $8 to $10 in rural areas, to $14 to $16 in urban areas. Wages are also determined by whether the job is a union job or not, rather than by skills.

Home health/personal aides often now call upon skills utilizing health-monitoring equipment as well as the traditional skills of light housework and assisting with personal hygiene. As with CNAs, though, these additional skills have not translated into significant wage gains.[95]

Warehouse/logistics workers have traditionally needed to be able to sort, load, and stack inventory as well as to operate forklift equipment. Today, they also need to be able to operate a computer in order to enter and check orders and to control the supply chain. Despite the additional computer skills, BLS data indicate that warehouse wages have increased little in the past decade and are still well below the knowledge economy jobs.[96]

The Movement to Increase Wages in Low-Wage Practical Economy Jobs

In just the past few years, the low wages in many practical-economy jobs have become a major political and policy issue. Politicians, television talking heads, and political activists, especially on the left, are regularly warning of the negative consequences of income inequality at conferences on inequality, op-ed pieces, and in books and academic papers.

They are finding a receptive audience, as polls show income inequality to be among the top political issues today.

Much of the discussion of income inequality is incomplete or inaccurate. For example, far from being a new phenomenon, income inequality has been growing in the United States (and other advanced economies) since the late 1970s. The Great Recession provided a brief respite from the widening gap, as it brought significant income losses at all levels, including among the 1 percent who derive much of their income from investments. Since the recession ended in 2010, the top 10 percent of wage earners have recovered their income losses more quickly than others.

Additionally, it is important to distinguish between income inequality and income mobility. Despite the long-term trend of income inequality, there continues to be considerable economic mobility for individual workers. In the early 2000s, a team of researchers led by economist Michael Dardia of the SPHERE Institute tracked the wage progress of 133,000 workers in California over the period of 1988 to 2000. More than half of the workers who started out earning the lowest 20 percent of wages advanced to a higher wage bracket by 2000.[97] This is consistent with other national studies, which show considerable movement by workers up (and down) the wage structure. An Urban Institute review of five separate mobility studies in the 1990s found all showing a significant degree of movement between income quintiles—slightly less than one half of individuals switching income quintiles over a five year period and 60 percent over a ten-year period.[98]

Far from ignoring the issue, government officials have rushed to take action. Task forces have been established and hearings held. A number of tax and income support policies have been enacted: the expansion of the earned income tax credit, and more recently the state and local minimum wage laws.[99]

The difficulty, of course, is that there is no easy fix. Low wages in practical-economy jobs are rooted in some of the same forces driving the breakdown in full-time employment noted in Chapter 7: globalization, technology, and immigration.[100]

The Autism Job Club is decidedly non-political. Our focus has been placing people in jobs.

But we know we do not exist apart from the broader economy. The low-wage dilemma is not exclusive to the autism community. But as it relates to our goal of independent living, neither is it apart from the community.

Part VI
Autism and Employment for the More Severely Impacted

17

AUTISM AND SUPPORTED WORK

AS NOTED EARLIER, autism is indeed a spectrum, and people on the spectrum demonstrate a range of abilities. Up to now our focus has been on the employment prospects of individuals who would not be considered the most severely affected. But what of adults with autism who are either non-verbal or have significant impairment in speech and language communication?

For most of the post-World War II period, this segment of the autism population was often sent to state-run institutions—up through the 1970s to the larger state mental institutions, and increasingly in the past few decades to the smaller community-based residential facilities. Those who lived with their families were largely kept at home or in day-care programs or were employed part-time at sheltered workshops.

Among this segment of the autism community, employment options are beginning to increase. Several new forms of supported work are slowly emerging: supported enterprises, both in the practical economy and in the Internet economy, supported work in staffing enterprises by autism agencies, and supported work in new forms of sheltered workshops.

Supported Micro-Businesses in the Practical Economy and the Internet Economy

In supported work, as in other forms of autism employment, parents often are at the forefront. Three cases of parents linked to our Autism Job Club suggest the possibilities in supported work related to micro-businesses.

Lou Vismara is the cardiologist and corresponding job club member in Sacramento, whom we met in Chapter 2. He left his cardiology practice in 2000 to work full-time on autism policies. His son Mark, born in 1993, was diagnosed at eighteen months of age with full-spectrum autism. In the past few years, Lou and his wife Wendy have dedicated themselves to finding employment for Mark and other adults similarly situated. Lou provides the following account of Mark's background and employment.

> Mark was born on April 19, 1993, following a completely uneventful pregnancy and delivery, as a completely healthy baby. During his first year of life, Mark frequently exceeded most of his developmental milestones. However, we became concerned when, during his second year of life, he did not begin using appropriate speech and language. As with so many other families, we were reassured by several pediatricians that "Boys always speak later than girls; that Mark has three sisters who are doing all of his talking for him; and that Einstein did not speak until the age of five." Despite implementing the doctors' recommendations that Mark engage in more "playdates" with other toddlers, his speech remained non-existent and we began to notice unusual physical activities such as "hand-flapping, body-rocking, and object-spinning."

> Over the years, Mark has received an array of therapies and interventions. For three years following his diagnosis we engaged in forty hours per week of home-based ABA therapy, subsequently we found that Mark demonstrated significant improvements with the "Pivotal Response Therapy" pioneered by Drs. Lynn and Bob

Koegel. However, despite some improvements in communication (Mark currently has limited functional speech), aggressive tantrums, destructive actions, and self-injurious behaviors (biting and severe "head banging") became increasingly difficult problems. Over the years, an assortment of medications and continued behavioral interventions and supports have significantly improved, but not completely eliminated, these behaviors.

Mark is now twenty-one years of age. For the past several years he has been living in his own home with all-inclusive staff supports. He is enrolled in a special education school, also supported by an aide, which provides instructional services to students with autism and related intellectual disorders. Next year Mark will graduate from this school with a certificate of completion of his educational program. The rest of his life awaits him.

My wife and I have been committed to doing everything we can so that Mark's future includes activities that are productive, give him a sense of accomplishment and self-esteem, and optimize his potential. These goals and objective are identical to the hopes and aspirations that we have for our "neurotypical" children.

Lou has developed a set of strategies for instructing Mark in vocational activities—which are summarized later in this chapter. These vocational tasks activities included mowing lawns and garden work, food preparation, and sorting and labeling donations for the Goodwill store.

Describing lawn mowing, Lou sets out five stages of introducing the task to Mark, dividing the task into discrete parts, modeling each of the discrete parts, and combining the discrete parts into the whole task. The lawn work started with the family lawn. It has expanded to Mark mowing the lawns of neighbors. Mark does not charge for his services. The hope is that the neighbors will value the service and be receptive to payment in the future. Mowing lawns is expanding to related garden work. As Lou explains,

In addition to mowing his lawn, Mark is also required to sweep all of his porch, walkways, and driveway; rake the leaves from his yard on a weekly basis; place the leaves (and other trash) in a recycling bind; deal appropriately with the bins' weekly curbside recycling process. We are also in the process of having Mark use an electric powered "leaf blower"—a somewhat more challenging process because of the associated loud noise. Not infrequently we also involve Mark in gardening chores such as weeding, removing shrubbery, or planting new flowers. Although these activities are presently being implemented strictly as "home care" adaptive life skills, these activities may also hold the potential for future vocational adaptation, such as landscape worker or other potential outdoor or gardening activities.

Food preparation is a second potential vocational activity that Lou is teaching Mark and that Mark is undertaking on a small basis. Mark not only prepares his own meals, but has also started "Mark's Eats & Treats," a food preparation activity by which twice a week Mark prepares and sells (for a very nominal fee) his sandwiches, salads, and other snacks to a predetermined number of the school staff. Lou adds,

> Along with the vocational preparation, Mark participates in community-based volunteer activities, at Goodwill Industries and at his church. At Goodwill, Mark volunteers several times each week in assisting in sorting, labeling and storing donations of clothing, shoes, and video tapes. Each weekend, Mark volunteers at a local church that serves a large regional congregation, placing donation cards and other information throughout the pews.

> We believe that these diverse activities not only enhance Mark's sense of self-worth and self-esteem, but enable Mark to participate as an important and contributing member of our family and our community. Furthermore, they enable Mark to gradually increase his circle of friends and supports as well as getting community members to become acquainted with Mark.

Lou and Wendy Vismara have refused to write off Mark as "unemployable" or institutionalize or warehouse him. Laura Shumaker is another of our job club parents who with her husband have eschewed institutionalization or warehousing and have invested a great amount of time and effort in carving out a work role for their son, Matthew. In Matthew's case, the Shumakers have turned to the unusual community of Camphill Communities to augment their own efforts in a gardening vocation for Matthew. Laura has written over the past decade about Matthew's challenges and development with an honesty that is very rare in the autism literature. In her book, *A Regular Guy: Growing Up with Autism*,[101] she presents in some detail Matthew's challenges throughout his elementary and high school, his rejections and sensitivity to these rejections, his inability to fit into the local community, and his violent behavior, which resulted in regular complaints from schools, from other parents, from the local police.

In the fall of 2003, Matthew transferred from the public high school in Lafayette, California, to Camphill Special School, a residential school in Pennsylvania. The school is part of Camphill Communities, a worldwide movement based on Christian ideals and the teachings of Rudolf Steiner. Over 100 Camphill residential sites have been established, bringing adults with learning disabilities and mental health problems "to live, learn, and work together with others in an atmosphere of mutual respect and equality."[102]

Matthew left Camphill School in 2008 (not with a diploma, but a "learning for life" certificate), and soon moved closer to home to Camphill California, a community for adults with learning disabilities on six acres of land near Santa Cruz. Since 2009, Matthew has lived at Camphill California and participated as a member of the land crew in gardening and landscaping and more recently in building repairs.

Matthew showed interest in lawn work as a child, and the Shumakers made efforts to support this interest, getting him a lawn mower when he was eleven. In his teenage years, while still living at home, Matthew began mowing, trimming, and blowing the yards of neighbor homes in Lafayette. At Camphill, Matthew is part of the gardening crew for the facility and neighboring facilities, for which he receives a small stipend.

According to Laura, his gardening work is very important to him. When he is at home he becomes restless if he does not have something productive to do. He wants to go to work as soon as he awakes in the morning. For the near future at least, the Shumakers plan to continue to help him find gardening customers in the neighborhood, as they work to enhance his construction and handyman skills.

In her *San Francisco Chronicle* blog, Laura recently wrote about Matthew's difficulties making any social connections, friends, and romantic relations. Recently, at age twenty-eight, he has started making connections, and is even speaking of possible romantic relations in hopeful, but realistic, terms. "There was a time when I thought that I could cultivate friendships—and more—for Matthew. I didn't believe he could do it himself. But Matthew has his own timetable, as do the rest of us."[103] This timetable extends to employment, as well as social relations.

Abe Tabas is a man in his twenties with autism whose parents have encouraged his art work and helped him set up a website to sell it. Abe grew up in San Francisco, where he still lives with his parents. For a time he attended an inclusion program for students with autism in the San Francisco Unified School District before transferring to Oak Hill, a Marin school that focuses on students with autism. He graduated from Oak Hill with a certificate of completion in June 2012, and entered the ARC day program. He attends the ARC daily, participating in classes and day activities with an individual aide.

Outside of ARC, his parents have encouraged him to pursue an interest in his drawing. In 2010, they set up a website for his drawings (www.ARTabas), to sell online. The website includes Abe's drawings for greeting cards (birthday cards, thank you cards, and holiday cards), prints, and images on clothing. The website describes him as an "autistic artist" and notes, "As an autistic person, Abe has faced many challenges in his life. He was also blessed with a strong talent for the visual arts."

In contrast to other autistic artists, such as Stephen Wiltshire, the drawings are not distinguished by elaborate detail and precision. Rather, as described by an ARC counselor, the drawings bring a child-like "directness and innocence" to their subjects. A good number of them are of animals: a bear family, a flamingo family, a bird, and cow. Others are of holiday scenes.

In a video presentation on the website, Abe describes art as his career. His mother Connie adds, "His work is now listed on a website that ARC has set up to market the art work of its clients ("Artists from the ARC") and a gym that is starting in the East Bay catering to persons with autism has asked for Abe's art to put on its walls. I see him expanding in the future to other art forms, especially to sculpture, which he loves."

Supported Work in Mainstream Workplaces

Terry Goodwin is the director of business development and partnerships at the ARC, where she has worked for over twenty-five years. She is in charge of ARC efforts to develop job placements in mainstream firms. This usually means convincing firms to at least try out workers with disabilities, who they wouldn't hire through the normal hiring processes. ARC serves the range of workers with disabilities, but, as noted in Chapter 4, adults with autism now comprise the greatest number of new clients

The ARC adults with autism themselves comprise a range of abilities and skills. The easiest to place are those who have significant language along with a high school degree (or, in rarer cases, college or college degrees). Sloan is a high school graduate with some post-secondary education at City College who was placed by ARC at Trader Joe's. He works three days a week as a bagger. John has a high school diploma and is a greeter at the Academy of Sciences, also part-time. Even these "higher functioning" adults with autism, though, usually require Terry and her staff to negotiate with employers and provide work supports for at least a few weeks or months in the form of a job coach.

What of the more severely impacted? Terry explains that the same principles of customized evaluation and work supports that apply to the "higher functioning" adults with autism apply to the more severely impacted. She and her staff will start with identifying skills and levels of support, as they do with other workers. Obviously, those who are more severely affected require higher levels of support and more time with job coaches. Terry notes, though, that "We try to find a work role for all, however impacted." Most placement success today is with placements in office facility set-up and clean-up staff for the city's rapidly expanding tech sector and the business services firms that serve them.

Additionally, ARC has developed a form of supported work for the more severely impacted that involves project-based tasks. ARC, as the subcontractor, acts as the employer of record. It has developed contracts with a major assisted-living facility to do laundry tasks, with the local convention industry to perform labeling and bagging of convention materials, and with the federal Department of Health and Human Services to arrange file folders. The work crews are sent on site to perform the tasks and are accompanied by job coaches. Though the employment is irregular, the ARC as employer does pay minimum wage and tries to use the assignments as evaluation opportunities for transitioning at some future time into more direct employment.[104]

Supported Work and the Sheltered Workshop

For over forty years, from the early 1960s, ARC operated a sheltered workshop (sometimes known as a "community workshop") for the more severely impacted. Like many sheltered workshops around the nation, it closed in the early 2000s, the result of both economics and policy shifts. But there are persons in the autism community who are already calling for its return.[105]

Jack Fagan was hired as an instructor at the ARC sheltered workshop in 1993 and in a few years became its director. He stayed until it closed in 2003. He regards the years he spent at the sheltered workshop as the most satisfying of his career. He is among those who believe it should return in some form.

In the early 1990s, Jack recalls that the ARC had around 100–120 clients at any time participating in the sheltered workshop located on the second floor of the ARC building. The ARC had contracts for assembling products and sorting/filling merchandise bags—for example with Leapfrog, then a major manufacturer of educational toys, and Jessica McClintock, the garment and fashion firm.

Payment was based on piece-work, with each worker paid on the number of products assembled or sorted/filled. Though some workers exceeded minimum wage, for most workers this meant a sub-minimum wage. Jack recalls,

> The sub-minimum wage was one factor that fueled opposition to the sheltered workshop approach, but there were others.
>
> Sheltered workshops were seen as isolating adults with disabilities in separate settings, limiting their social relations with other adults. The prevailing idea became inclusion of workers, including the severely impacted, in mainstream work sites.
>
> Some of the criticisms of sheltered workshops were accurate. But ending these sheltered workshops did not result in mainstream employment for former employees, especially the more severely impacted. Most of the adults I worked with at the ARC sheltered workshop did not find subsequent employment in mainstream firms and have been largely unemployed since.
>
> Further, the sheltered workshop had its own social connections. It enabled adults with severe disabilities to get out of their houses and gave them somewhere to go each day. Friendships and connections grew between workers at the sheltered workshops, and between the instructors/job coaches and the workers. Being with the people at the sheltered workshops was certainly the best job I've had.

Corey Azevedo is another San Francisco Bay Area veteran of the sheltered workshop who believes it can have a future, with variations on the traditional model. With an academic background in cultural anthropology, including a master's degree from the University of Sussex, Corey was a staff member of several sheltered workshops in Northern California in the 2000s and continues to write about their role. He argues that the workshops should be transformed into worker cooperatives, empowering the workers as owners to elect the workshop management. "In the cooperative model the disability community builds assets, takes control over business operations, and gains bargaining power in relation to service providers. The approach is entrepreneurial, empowering, and achievable. Most importantly, 14(c) workers making subminimum wages becoming coowners receiving dividends."[106] (14(c) workers are defined under the Fair Labor Standards Act as having "a disability for the job being performed.")

Nationwide, the direction of academic and practitioner research and writing continues to argue for moving individuals away from sheltered workshops and transitioning them into mainstream employment. The New York Makes Work Pay Initiative, funded by the U.S. Department of Health and Human Services, is one of the main national study groups on employment for workers with disabilities. The Initiative has resulted in several published papers on the transformation of center-based work into mainstream employment. These papers argue that the government costs per participant are less in mainstream employment than in sheltered employment, while financial and social values are greater. They also set out a road map for the transformation.[107]

But like earlier discussions of ending sheltered workshops, New York Makes Work Pay glosses over the difficulties of locating employment in the mainstream workforce, especially the difficulties for the most severely impacted. Further, the two approaches—mainstream employment and sheltered workshops—are not exclusive. The focus of employment for the severely impacted, as for other workers with autism, can continue to be mainstream employment. Few in the autism community would disagree with this. But the sheltered workshop can exist as one additional option.

Part VII
Lifelong Learning, Workplace Culture, and the Future of the Autism Job Club

18

AUTISM, RETRAINING, AND LIFELONG LEARNING

THE U.S. ECONOMY is changing. Most workers now need to train and retrain for several occupations over a lifetime. Lifelong learning and the need to continually refresh skills are now part of the employment landscape.

For adults with autism, retraining and lifelong learning are as relevant as for other workers. Adults with autism and their advocates need to be aware of the extensive retraining network that is arising in the U.S., both public and private, or risk being left behind.

The Extensive Retraining Network and the Public Workforce System

An extensive public-sector retraining system has arisen in the past two decades. Retraining and reemployment services are now available to all laid-off workers through local Workforce Investment Boards (WIBs), in order to help these workers transition into new employment.

For most of the forty years following the enactment of the 1962 Manpower Development Training Act—the first of the major postwar federal workforce initiatives—the public workforce system focused on two populations seen as having greatest barriers to employment: young people entering the labor market and unemployed adults with limited work history.[108] In the past decade, federal job-training money and focus has shifted to include the "dislocated worker," the worker laid off as part of a plant closing, major company downsizing, or layoff due to reduced company revenues. The 2013 DOL budget for training and employment programs included $1.2 billion for dislocated worker training and placement, compared to $829 million and $771 million in the traditional categories of youth activities and adult activities. In addition, the DOL budget included an additional $500 million in Trade Adjustment Assistance Career Training for dislocated workers, whose layoffs were tied to global competition.[109]

Hundreds of studies are undertaken each year on effective job training and retraining. Yet, the elements of effective training are straightforward and haven't changed much over the years.[110] Four elements stand out: (i) training tailored to individual skills, (ii) training tried to the number of job openings in the immediate area, (iii) training curriculum developed with local employers; and (iv) as much as possible, employer commitment to hire prior to training. None of these elements is complex. The better retraining programs are those that excel in implementation.

To a great extent the retraining system in most communities incorporates these elements. Training doesn't always lead to employment. But most WIBs and community colleges and other training providers are careful to link training to the skills and interests of the individual worker and to the number of jobs likely to be available in a region.

The retraining/reemployment system has been most conspicuous in recent years following large plant closings. In August 2009, Toyota announced the closing of the New United Motors Manufacturing Inc. (NUMMI) automobile plant in Fremont, California, and the layoff of 4,700 workers. The retraining/reemployment system immediately went into place. The NUMMI Reemployment Center was established, a project of the local Alameda County Workforce Investment Board and the United Auto Workers.

Each worker who participated (participation was voluntary) had their skills and interests evaluated. Would the worker be willing to relocate to Toyota plants in other states? Would she or he be willing to move for a manufacturing job in other areas of California? What skills did the worker possess that might be transferable to other occupations and sectors? Was the worker willing to go through a retraining program for a new occupation in say health care, or transportation/ logistics or trucking, to name a few of the occupations with openings in the region? Each worker was eligible for up to $15,000 in reimbursed retraining costs, along with continued receipt of unemployment insurance benefits.

A small number of the workers did take the opportunity to move to Toyota plants in other states. The great majority of ex-NUMMI workers sought to stay in the Bay Area and tried to find another job right away or retrain for a new career. The retraining ranged across occupations. Auto mechanic and machine operator were two popular occupations for retraining. But there also was retraining at the local community colleges and private proprietary schools, in such fields as pharmacy technician, medical technician, dental laboratory technician, welder, and trucker.

Over the next few years, placements for the workers lagged behind expectations. Hiring overall in the region's economy remained slow; many of the workers had not looked for jobs in years; math and reading levels were often below tenth grade. Still, the subsidized retraining options were generous and recognized that the workers in nearly all cases did not have the option of remaining in auto manufacturing, no matter how comfortable or competent they had become. They needed to retool.

A similar extensive retraining process took place a few years later when the nearby Solyndra solar panel plant closed in August 2011. Within hours of the announced closing, the Alameda County WIB was on site, distributing flyers about reemployment and retraining options for the 1,100 workers laid off. Placement and retraining options were tailored to each worker based on interests and skills. Reemployment was more successful than at NUMMI, since nearby technology employers valued the light manufacturing and software engineering skills among the workforce. But also workers trained for new careers as medical assistants, supply chain managers, HVAC technicians, and dialysis technicians.

While plant closures receive the most attention, the retraining system is increasingly available to any laid off worker. The process is tailored to individual interests and the jobs available in the region. Here's the process at the NOVA WIB in Silicon Valley.

Any worker laid off is eligible for dislocated worker services, without regard to income; to be certified, the worker must only show some evidence of lay-off, such as the letter from the employer announcing the layoff. The certification process is streamlined to a day or so, and the worker is assigned to a career advisor. The career advisor presents options for reemployment assistance. Most workers need assistance in updating a résumé, and accessing the rapidly-changing Internet job board system. The NOVA job club, ProMatch, is presented as an option, as is instruction in the online networking opportunities.

Further, short-term skills-upgrading seminars are often a part of the reemployment process. NOVA counts a good number of laid off technology workers among its enrollees: not only engineers but also marketing managers, human resources staff, communications staff, and business services staff in tech firms. Specialized seminars are offered to marketing professionals in the latest marketing computer software or to human resources professionals in the requirements of the Affordable Care Act or other workplace guidelines. The goal is to be most current in the skills that employers are seeking.

In some cases, the worker will conclude that he or she needs to seek a new occupation. The same retraining options that were available to the NUMMI and Solyndra workers are made available now to other laid-off workers. NOVA will subsidize retraining for a new career, especially when the job seeker has been unemployed more than twenty-six weeks and has undertaken an exhaustive job search.

Community colleges are becoming a new center of retraining and reemployment efforts.[111] Community college employer advisory groups are being strengthened, job placement staff added, contract education expanded.

In California, for example, the community college system is home to 112 community colleges, which in 2009–2010 enrolled more than 2.7 million Californians. It is the largest system of public higher education in the United States. The system dates back to 1907 when state legislation enabled high schools to create "junior colleges" to provide academic courses beyond high school for local students, often with the goal of helping them advance to four year universities. Like many of California's institutions, the system exploded in size in the post World War II period. The California Master Plan for Higher Education in 1960 formally recognized the California community colleges as part of the higher education system with the University of California and California State College systems.[112]

Since the early 1960s, the system has had a mix of missions, including assisting students to gain skills and earn college credits to transfer to a four year university, assisting students to earn a professional certificate and/or associate's degree, and providing training or retraining for immediate job placement. These missions have jockeyed for prominence among the California community colleges, and continue to do so today. In the past five years, several statewide task forces have been established and studies commenced to consider how the community colleges should balance these missions and allocate resources.[113]

The retraining role consistently is singled out by these task forces. The vision is of community colleges that workers can come back to at various points in their careers, to refresh skills or develop new ones.[114] The vocational offerings already are numerous: the

California community colleges currently offer certificates and degrees in 175 occupations.

The community colleges are giving particular attention in retraining to the "new technician" occupations: medical technician, information technology technician, automotive technician. These are occupations for which training can often be done in a year or less. They also are occupations which pay "decent wages" (above $15 an hour), and which combine routine technical tasks with problem solving and cannot be easily automated.[115]

Internet Retraining and Lifelong Learning Outside of the Public Workforce System

Developing largely outside of the government-funded workforce system is a system of Internet-based retraining. Each week brings new Internet job training/retraining companies, competing to offer a retraining process that offers more effective interactive education or personalized services or a better fit with jobs opening.[116]

Empowered.com, Metrix Learning, and LearnUp are three of the new wave of retraining, each with its own target occupations and length of training. Empowered.com was founded in 2011, headed by two of California's leading technology and entertainment entrepreneurs, Steve Poizner and Sherry Lansing, and backed by $15 million in venture capital funds. It is a partnership with the University of California, Los Angeles Extension program, with a fully online training. The program is oriented toward iPad use and advertised as "a revolutionary learning environment which places instructors, mentors, and fellow students just one touch away—anytime and anywhere."

The Empowered.com training came online in October 2012 and consists of UCLA Extension Certificates in five occupational categories: Project Management, IT Management, Global Sustainability, Health Care Management and Patient Advocacy. Each certificate in turn consists of eight classes, with the expectation that the student will take two classes per quarter over a four-quarter year period. Though Empowered.com is open to all persons over eighteen, the majority of the first enrollees are over forty years of age and seeking a new career.

Metrix Learning focuses on shorter-term skills upgrading (twenty to one hundred hours) for laid off workers, often "just-in-time" skills to meet specific job requirements. It offers online courses, for example, in Microsoft Office Specialist, QuickBooks, Cisco, and Six Sigma.

LearnUp targets skills in entry level jobs in sales, customer service, and related areas for major employers, such as Staples, Gap, and Safeway. Job seekers who want to apply for jobs with these employers are asked to complete short training videos posted on the LearnUp website. Staples, for example, has posted a training video on sales techniques for job seekers applying to be an "Easy Technology Associate" with Staples. By watching this video and other videos on sales, the job seeker signals basic competencies and interest in Staples and his application is flagged.

Beyond online training/retraining are the more general on-line education Massively Open Online Courses, or MOOCs. Chief among these today are Udacity, Coursera, and Khan Academy. These sites offer a wide range of educational courses, in most cases at no cost and on demand. The courses include thousands of college-level courses in the sciences, humanities, and social sciences as well as courses to pursue almost any vocational or avocational interest: filmmaking, art history, long distance running, sculpture, astronomy, preparing for the SAT.

At present, each of these MOOCs provides a different learning approach. At Khan Academy, the student logs on and can choose from 3,600 video seminars to watch at his or her own pace. Udacity is slightly more structured like a college course, with an instructor who builds a syllabus. With Udacity there are discussion boards for students to interact and a final exam to obtain a certificate. Coursera is the most structured, partnering with universities to offer online courses through the Coursera site. These are formal courses with a professor, syllabus, video class time, homework, and a set of deadlines.

So far, the MOOCs are not focused on job placement or on training or retraining. But they too are evolving rapidly, adding certifications that are tied to the work world and developing course offerings in concert with employers.

Autism, Retraining, and Lifelong Learning

What is the connection of MOOCs or any of the other retraining and skills upgrading tools to adults with autism?

John Comegys is a long time vocational counselor, who volunteers with the job club. Like Jan Johnston-Tyler and Cindy Zoeller, Comegys did not set out to be an autism job coach, but has found himself drawn to the autism community. Comegys graduated from Pacific University in Oregon in 1973 and earned a master's degree in rehabilitation counseling from Fresno State. He had a lengthy career as a teacher and vocational rehabilitation counselor before deciding a few years ago to be a job coach for adults with autism. He drives from Dixon, California, each month to assist in job club activities. He uses many of the same skills he gained as a vocational counselor, but modifies them to address the additional level of services needed by most of our adults with autism.

As a vocational counselor, Comegys advised workers on career changes, both voluntary and involuntary. The voluntary changes might come from a desire to make a career change; the involuntary changes from a layoff or injury.

Comegys believes that adults with autism need to be as active in refreshing skills and adapting new skills as other workers, perhaps more so. He spreads his arms out wide to indicate the range of skills and abilities among adults with autism, ranging from those with advanced degrees to those who have no speech. All or nearly all of these adults have a capacity to learn well beyond their youth. "I checked recently with the DSM-5 under Autism Prognosis and it says it is typical for learning and compensation to continue throughout life."

Persons learn at different speeds, and this is true of adults with autism. Some may be able to master as adults skills that they were not able to master as youth. Others may never be able to master certain, say, reading or math skills (they may never get beyond eighth grade reading or math levels or below) but have the capacity to gain job related skills. Further, that part of the autism community who lack social communication and emotional intelligence skills have the capacity to learn these skills as they age. "I'm counseling two adults with autism who have gone back to school to update their technical skills, and a third who is registering for classes. Other clients of mine are continuing to improve their social skills and social cognition through workshops and practice."

"Time is on our side," Comegys likes to say. By this, in part, he means that as the numbers of adults with autism increases, public policy is more likely to change. He also means that adults with autism will be able to master at least some skills that as youth they lagged behind others. As a vocational counselor he knows that adults with autism surprise in their pace of learning and their ability to learn.

19

AUTISM AND WORKPLACE CULTURE

THE GREAT MAJORITY of efforts in autism employment today focus on the technical and social skills needed by workers to find and hold jobs. But there is an alternate approach that is being pursued by a handful of autism employment groups. Though less developed and more indirect than the placement and training strategies, it can complement these strategies.

This approach involves changing the mainstream workplace culture. One part of this change involves more active recruitment of adults with autism. A second part involves creating a culture that instills greater patience for adults with autism to master the specific work tasks and procedures and flexibility in regard to unusual or odd behaviors of adults with autism.

Marcia Scheiner of the Asperger Syndrome Training & Employment Partnership (ASTEP), based in New York, is one of the autism employment advocates who is taking the lead on this approach. ASTEP was founded by Scheiner in 2010. She had previously had spent twenty-five years in the financial sector, with a number of major banks and insurance companies. She has a son with autism, who was nineteen in 2010, and she saw a gap as she researched the employment services for adults with autism.

These employment services focused on preparing adults with autism to try to be competitive in job placement and fit into the existing work environments. In her view, this would always be an uphill climb. An accompanying strategy needed to be employer-focused: encouraging major employers to actively seek out workers with autism, and develop a culture that better leveraged the focus and talents of adults with disabilities. As Scheiner explains,

> The focus of most autism programs is on preparing the individuals, on the supply side, in job placement and retention. The need I saw was on the demand side, of awareness and training with companies. ASTEP does not place individuals; instead we concentrate on the employer side, to create the environment for outreach and hiring.
>
> Job placement services are vital to the success of the individual, but the employer needs to be equally prepared to manage the individual on the spectrum. I like to think of the support needs as a two-way street, with the employee on the spectrum and the employer meeting halfway.
>
> Recent studies show that over 30 percent of adults with Asperger's syndrome have some post-secondary education. The supply exists; we need to influence the demand.

ASTEP began by giving presentations to industry groups and industry conferences, and offering staff training to individual companies. Scheiner drew on her contacts and on the connections to autism of human resources officials with major companies.

In the summer of 2011, Scheiner added meetings with human resources, accompanied by ten to twelve young adults with autism, to "put a face" on autism. Rather than pitch an autism employment initiative to human resources staff, Scheiner asked the staff to help the young adults understand the work world of employers. In her experience, human resources staff frequently will organize such meetings for a variety of outside groups.

Through these meetings, Scheiner took the opportunity to talk about the advantages that adults with autism can bring to an employer, particularly higher loyalty and greater focus. She also talked about the good-will and marketing benefits of hiring from the growing autism community. She talked about the patience that might be needed and time for adjustment to the job. She sought in her words to "demystify autism for the employers and to let them see firsthand the skill sets individuals on the spectrum can bring to the workplace."

She adds of these meetings, "Human resources staff consistently are impressed by the seriousness of our young adults, their desire to work, and their insights. We have been able to follow up with these companies to link them to the local autism job placement agencies and job counselors." ASTEP started with employers in New York and is expanding to other states.[117]

The vision of a workplace more favorable to adults with autism is shared by a wide group of autism advocates, parents, and adults with autism.[118] In speaking of this more favorable workplace, the advocates generally embrace three common themes.

The first theme is more active recruitment of adults with autism. The vision: employers going beyond the general hiring processes, such as the job boards and structured interviews, to seek out adults with autism and the autism employment agencies. Several major retail employers, including Walgreens and Best Buy, have active autism recruitment efforts (Chapter 16), as do a few technology firms (Chapter 11). These firms, though, represent a very small number at present.

The second theme is patience in providing time for adults with autism to master work processes. Nearly all workers need opportunity to adapt to a new work environment. But adults with autism generally need greater patience than others. Tasks can be learned, but may require a longer period of adjustment. Autism coach Cindy Zoeller explains, "In my experience, if given sufficient time, adults with autism usually can master the jobs they are hired for, and over time prove to be more focused and willing to stick with the job than other workers." The vision: such patience will be the rule, not the exception.

The third theme is flexibility by employers in adapting to unusual behaviors. "We try to find workplaces and employers who will tolerate unusual behaviors," the ARC's Terry Goodwin notes, and singles out as welcoming workplaces the new bohemia of tech firms and the business services firms catering to them. The vision: such flexibility becomes a practice widespread among employers.

How realistic is this vision or series of visions for workplace culture shifts? What would it take to begin to achieve these shifts? The recent experiences of autism advocates suggest several lessons for implementation, summarized below.

- *Changing workplace culture is a firm-by-firm effort*: To speak of changing workplace culture generally is misleading. There is no general workplace culture; there are the individual cultures of thousands of major employers. Impacts will be on a firm-by-firm basis.

- *Success in a small number of firms will spur impacts in other firms*: As with so many other areas of social policy, demonstrated impact in a few firms is the best approach for stimulating impacts in other firms. "Before anything else, we need to show employers examples of successful implementation among the tech industry," Brian Jacobs explains of his efforts to achieve greater hiring and patience among technology employers. "Employers will respond to results, however initial, rather than theory." Marcia Scheiner notes that in ASTEP's experience there is a "competitive aspect": employers are drawn to come onboard as they see their competitors participating and finding success.

- *Identifying a marketing advantage with an "autism friendly" workplace*: "'You should do,' doesn't get you very far in influencing employer behavior," states Dr. Lou Vismara, drawing on his past attempts to spur hiring and retention. In his view, companies need to see a business reason, a financial gain, both to be more aggressive in hiring and to make other culture shifts. Dr. Vismara sees this financial gain in the increased customer loyalty and marketing edge for businesses that hire and retain adults with autism. "Businesses today emphasize 'green' values and local-grown/local-made values to get a marketing advantage. To be able to say that a business is actively hiring and retaining adults with autism can similarly be a marketing edge."

- *Documenting the greater loyalty and higher performance of adults with autism*: In her meetings with employers, Marcia Scheiner speaks of reduced turnover and higher performance among adults with autism. As we have seen in previous chapters, similar claims have been made by founders of autism-focused businesses and parent advocates behind hiring initiatives at major employers. Yet, the attempts to document this greater loyalty and higher performance are rare: the Walgreens distribution plant study is among the few. There are reasons to think that the greater loyalty and higher performance are present but so far the argument is mainly theory. Wider documentation is required to make a convincing case to employers.

***

Workplace cultures have been developed by firms over time, reflecting the accumulated experience of the rules and processes that are most effective in an industry. So the cultures are not easy to change—nor should they be. At the same time, these cultures do shift with both economic and social changes. Autism advocates have achieved some small shifts in recent years. Like the other autism employment strategies, this strategy will be one of incremental gains, built on documented examples of market advantage, worker loyalty, and worker productivity.

20

THE FUTURE OF THE AUTISM JOB CLUB

WHERE DO WE go from here?

Let's start by catching up with the job club members who attended our organizing meeting in November 2011.

A snapshot in late 2014 finds various employment outcomes, as would be expected. Paul is continuing his handyman business (along with pursuing his mountain climbing avocation) and Greg has a similar business. Along with Stacey and her pet-sitting business, they are part of our self-employed contingent—all of whom are still searching to grow beyond marginal enterprises.

Alex, who was unemployed in November 2011, was able by 2013 to secure a job as a substitute para-professional with the San Francisco Unified School District. (His degree in child/adolescent education paid off.) He continues today in this position and continues to interview for a full-time para-professional position. Andrew has settled into his mix of a two-days-a-week recycling position with his pillow design and sculpturing. But he still comes to the club. So too does Jim Ullrey, now seventy-five, who on his own found a part-time job assembling furniture on a contract basis for stores and for private customers.

Martha and Gabe have not come to the job club for some time. With the help of a counselor at the state Department of Rehabilitation, Martha found a job as a para-legal and her father (who does come to club meetings) reports that she continues to be employed today. Gabe is still looking, doing a little part-time proof-reading and editing work on a contract basis. Mark is still looking to restart a business in information technology, while also being open to all forms of employment.

Daniel was another of the early club members. In early 2012, club facilitator Cindy Zoeller identified Daniel as having very sophisticated, near savant, computer skills. Cindy spent a lot of time with him, identifying job leads. She reports, though, that he's been unable to pursue a serious job search of going to interviews or pursuing projects on time or following up.[119]

This is only a snapshot. Job situations can and do change overnight. But as this brief glimpse shows, despite all of the publicity that autism has received since 2011, despite autism's heightened role in popular culture since 2011, employment for adults with autism remains irregular, fragile, and marginal. A good portion of the adult autism community remains warehoused in adult day programs or at home. This is especially true for adults with autism without family members who can continuously monitor and assist with employment and reemployment.

Meanwhile at the job club, we experiment with expanding our employment services. Our early efforts to expand, including the online Spectrum Employment Network and the software testing training group, Specialists Guild, have been augmented by other networking and technology employment efforts.

Brian Jacobs recently took a sabbatical from his venture capital firm, Emergence Capital. Using his own funds, he traveled to Western Europe and visited the technology firms focused on employing adults with autism: Specialisterne in Denmark, Passwerks in Belgium, Auticon in Germany, as well as the SAP headquarters in Germany.

Our autism technology employment network with Bay Area technology firms has not gained traction over the past three years, and he's determined to move it forward.

Camilla and Greg connected with the SAP hiring initiative in Palo Alto and are volunteering as advisors. One of our club members, Janice, is among the first seven trainees.

Keith Halperin, an executive recruiter who identifies on the autistic spectrum, has stepped forward to volunteer as a one-to-one job coach. Laura Shumaker continues to research and profile autism employment initiatives on her *San Francisco Chronicle* autism blog. On the state level, Dr. Lou Vismara is coordinating upcoming hearings by the California State Senate on employment for adults with autism.[120]

Our Individual Job Search Strategies

As word of the club has spread in the past two years, I have received emails from adults with autism and an even greater number from family members, asking for employment assistance. I try to respond to each request within the same day—as a parent, I am well aware of the deep worry that lies behind each message.

If a job seeker is in San Francisco or the inner Bay Area, I will try to suggest potential employers or offer to brainstorm approaches. I will ask them to email me regularly about companies they have contacted and try to make suggestions or follow up if I know anyone at the company. Usually, if a job seeker just knows that someone else is interested or tracking her or his job search, that can be a significant motivator in itself—to overcome the discouragement that defines job search today.

For others in the autism community outside of the Bay Area, my advice is often more general, along the following lines.

The starting point for your job search as an adult with autism or a family member, should be the same as for all job seekers: identifying and emphasizing strengths and interests. Don't think of particular occupations for persons with autism. To be sure, some segment of our autism community will be skilled in technology jobs, but a very limited segment.

Find a job coach to work with you, if possible, either privately or through the government-sponsored placement system. Also, if possible, find a job coach who is knowledgeable about placing adults with autism. Such a job coach will use the same tools as other job coaches but be skilled in teaching and adapting these skills.

Perhaps most of all recognize how more difficult it is today for all job seekers than it was in previous decades. Ignore the official government job numbers that show the national economy continuing to improve. It has recovered the depths of the Great Recession in 2008–2010, when the economy was shrinking and net job losses were in the millions. But the overall numbers mask the breakdown of some full-time jobs into part-time, contingent, and project-based employment.

Following this, you need submit many more applications than was true in the past. You need to go way beyond the job boards, with supplemental information and in-house recommendations, if possible. Further, you need to try to "get in the door" in any way, through taking a lower level job, if necessary, or by volunteering.

Within the autism community there is disagreement about whether to "disclose" autism during the hiring process. I side with autism job coach, Jan Johnston Tyler and others, that it is almost always best to do so. Given how widely is autism's reach in our society, most employers will have some connection. They are more than likely to provide the needed patience and flexibility if they know from the start.

Finally, I will add, please join our collective autism community efforts. We cannot rely on government. America has long been a society of voluntary associations and extra-government groups to get things done.[121] The autism community already is rich with voluntary associations. We need to build on these associations—on the in-person associations and online associations—such as WrongPlanet and AutisticsSpeak.[122] At the center of our collective efforts will be the voice of adults with autism themselves—"nothing about us, without us," as the community motto goes.

Our Collective Employment Strategies

In this book we have set out an agenda for our collective efforts, based on recent autism employment experiences. Let us now return to the six main elements of this collective agenda and briefly review.

1. *The autism job coach*: Our collective efforts start with expanding the pool of autism job coaches—job coaches with expertise to teach and tailor the best job search strategies today for adults with autism. This expansion will include but not be limited to professionals. Adults with autism, family members, and advocates should be encouraged to invest the time to master job search skills for adults with autism. There is no secret knowledge. To a degree, we should all strive to be autism job coaches.

2. *The autism technology advantage*: Some portion of the community does perform well in technology jobs, especially software testing. The stand-alone businesses for software testing in the United States have not proved viable. But promise does lie in placements in major software companies, such as undertaken with much fanfare in 2014 by the German software company SAP, and with less publicity by the information technology firm Computer Aid and mortgage lender Freddie Mac. The process will be a slow one, the numbers in any firm will be small. But as is already being seen, successful autism employment placements in technology will spur additional placements.

3. *Autism and accessing the emerging Internet economy*: The Internet economy offers employment opportunities—in technology, marketing, administration jobs—directly in the social media and Internet commerce firms that have grown since 2011—as well as the thousands of start-up firms that

continue to arise each month. But its greater impact for autism employment will be in three other areas linked to this Internet economy: (1) the opportunities for micro-enterprises started by adults with autism to market themselves or form autism business collectives for joint marketing, business strategy, administration; (2) the opportunities for adults with autism to participate in the share economy, utilizing conventional goods and services or more unusual skills they might possess; and (3) the opportunities to tap into crowdfunding options now on such crowdfunding sites as Kiva, Kickstarter, and Indiegogo, especially targeting individual lenders who want to support autism employment.

4. *Autism, the practical economy and craft*: The majority of jobs in the next decade will not be in technology or even in the "knowledge economy." They will be the practical economy of bakers, car wash detailers, warehousepersons, retail clerks, bakers, health aides, and customer service representatives, to name a few of these occupations. Throughout the United States, parents of and advocates for adults with autism are starting businesses to directly employ adults with autism in the practical economy. Offering wider employment impacts, established practical economy firms, such as Walgreens and Best Buy, have launched targeted employment initiatives for adults with autism. To build on these initiatives and generate many others means a focus on the value of craft. Recent experiences suggest adults with autism can bring a craft to these jobs, especially an attention to detail, above the general population, as well as lower job turnover in these jobs. The concept of craft has made a comeback in the United States since 2000, particularly in the unexpected popularity of the work reality television shows. Craft and competitive advantage, not social good, will be the starting points in advocating for adults with autism in the practical economy.

5. *Autism and supported employment*: Most of the employment activity for adults with autism is focused on adults with Asperger's syndrome or other "high functioning" adults with autism. But there is no reason that those near the entire range of adults with autism, including the more severely impacted, should not have some form of employment or activity beyond adult day care. Today, unless a highly resourceful and relentlessly persistent parent is involved, such purposeful activity does not occur, and warehousing is most widespread. Updated thinking and focus on this segment of our autism community is called for, not only an updating of the sheltered workshop in renewed and revised forms, but more so with inclusion in mainstream workplaces.

6. *Autism, lifelong learning and workplace culture*: The American economy is becoming an economy of retraining for several occupations over a lifetime and of ongoing skills refreshment. For adults with autism, retraining is as relevant as for other workers. Adults with autism should be directed toward the same paths of lifelong learning as other workers. Further, within the mainstream workplaces, adults with autism are now counseled to adapt their behaviors with workplace culture. While this counseling needs to continue, the converse counseling in shifting workplace culture is needed. Existing workforce culture needs to be pushed to be more flexible—less impatient and less unforgiving—in the many cases it can do so without reducing quality performance (in many cases, increasing quality). There is a movement in the autism community to change workplace culture to accommodate adults with autism, and it is growing, as it should.

Public Service Employment for Adults with Autism

Beyond these six strategies, there is another that should call forth consideration: a form of direction job creation in the public sector, targeted at adults with autism, and structured as transitional employment. We have not included it in the six strategies that are the focus of this book as there are no good examples to point to today and it is not part of the policy discussion. But it should be, especially as it can be tied to reductions in the cost of government benefits, especially SSI and SSDI.

Public-service employment on a large scale was last tried under the Comprehensive Employment and Training Act (CETA) program of the 1970s. Government money was used to directly create jobs in local governments and in non-profits, targeted at the unemployed. Launched in 1977, CETA public service employment grew rapidly to 725,000 in jobs in 1978, the peak of job generation. It quickly declined, though, and ended in early 1981, amidst widespread criticism that the jobs were distributed based on politics and not need, and most of all that they were make-work—unfair to taxpayers and even to other workers in low wage jobs, who were not being subsidized.

A great deal has been written about Public Service Employment under CETA. Walter Shapiro, an aide to Secretary of Labor Ray Marshall when the program was developed, captures the view of many researchers and observers. Looking back in 2009, he agreed that the program should have been ended, that it was arrogantly and poorly administered without concern for taxpayers, and that it poisoned the well for other future public sector employment.[123]

Indeed, when President Obama and his team assembled the elements of the federal stimulus program in 2009 (the American Recovery and Reinvestment Act), public service employment was pointedly avoided. The stimulus program was built around "shovel ready" projects that could create or retain jobs primarily in private sector firms, on projects that were supposedly vetted. Any future attempt to create jobs in the public sector must navigate a very difficult path of implementation. It must address the higher costs of public sector employment versus disability benefits, the opposition by public sector unions to taking work away from their members, and the strong bureaucratic tendencies to reject bringing in persons from outside the civil service system.

Yet, there are reasons to pursue and try to develop the public-service employment—the main reason being the slow process of implementation that should be expected for the other six strategies. The moral argument needs to be made concerning why public-service employment should be targeted at adults with autism. Further, the difficult implementation issues noted above need to be carefully considered, as do implementation issues regarding the jobs as transitional employment. However, it's time that public-service employment reenter the policy discussion in relation to adults with autism and other disabilities as one of several employment strategies.

The Mix of Anger, Humor, and Perspective Going Forward

In 1973 Josh Greenfeld published *A Child Called Noah*, about his then seven-year-old son Noah, a boy with autism who had very little speech or purposeful activity. Greenfeld introduces Noah in the first chapter by noting, "His main activities are lint catching, thread pulling, blanket sucking, spontaneous giggling, inexplicable crying, eye squinting, wall-hugging, circle-walking, bed-bouncing, and incoherent babbling addressed to his finger-flexing right hand." The book chronicles Noah's behaviors through age five, and the efforts of the other Greenfelds (dad Josh, mom Foumi, and brother Karl) as the family tries to carve out a life for Noah and for themselves. Two subsequent books, *A Place for Noah* (1978) and *A Client Called Noah* (1986), continue the chronicle through 1980—and in an epilogue in the third book through 1985.

The Greenfelds try various schools, including starting their own school with other parents of autistic children. They try developmental therapists, nutritional therapists, physical therapists, and Dr. Ivar Lovaas's autism clinic in Los Angeles. In the end, none of these yield significant outcomes. At age nineteen, Noah, according to his father, remains without language and given to tantrums. Josh Greenfeld writes, "In many ways for all the attention and energy expended on him all these years, Noah at nineteen-and-a-half does not appear to have changed significantly in terms of his special behavioral and communication problems. At best, his I.Q. still measures at the level of an eighteen month old infant. At his worst, he is still given to . . . sudden rages that include spitting and clutching."

As he gets older, Noah is institutionalized for fifteen years, between the ages of twenty-five and forty, at Fairview Mental Hospital in Orange County, a state facility. Since 2006, he has been part of California's Regional Center system, living in a group home in South Central Los Angeles for adults with disabilities. He has never gained significant language.[124]

The Noah trilogy is worth reading today not because it gives us strategies for employment or behavior. It doesn't. What it does is convey the sensibility that should guide us in autism employment efforts going forward: a mix of anger, humor, and honesty.

Greenfeld is angry at the government bureaucracies, whom he sees as satisfied with warehousing Noah; and even more angry at the professionals for whom Noah is a source of revenue or a subject for research. His anger drives him to take the time to assemble his remarkable chronicle of Noah and his family, and to pilot educational approaches. But anger is not enough in public policy.

What Greenfeld does is mix anger with humor and perspective. He is able to see beyond the individual circumstances of Noah and the personalities of the government officials. He is able to see that there may be no "solution" for Noah, even as he understands that the current situation for Noah and other persons with autism is not sustainable.

Hundreds of memoirs by parents of children with autism have been published since the Noah Trilogy. Most are filled with tacked-on upbeat endings, or with children with autism being "cured," or with indignant complaints that government is "not doing anything." Greenfeld does not wrap up the story of either Noah or his family in a

Hollywood ending and does not look vaguely to government or politics, even as his story inspires us to greater thought and action.

I have read the trilogy several times. Every few years I reread parts of it.

Where We Go From Here

The past week has been an active one for the Autism Job Club.

At the job club meeting last Saturday, Greg Yates, our cochair, made a presentation on a recent visit to France. He and his partner, Anne-Laure, a woman with autism who grew up in France, toured various facilities for children and for adults with autism and met with autism groups.

Greg found the French autism community to be fifteen to twenty years behind the United States in autism inclusion. France has a budding autism movement, "Vaincre l'Autisme" (Defeating Autism) for treatment and inclusion and increased parent involvement. But Greg found disturbing the continued focus on psychoanalysis as a "cure" for autism and a still-prevalent view of autism as a psychological condition. Anne Laure thought she had survived only because she "escaped to America." Greg concluded his presentation with, "We were so happy to get back to America."

Brian Jacobs is back from his research trip to Western Europe, and organizing a gathering of tech companies regarding employment opportunities for our members. He's also hired an intern to build our LinkedIn employment group.

Additionally, the club has become part of two nascent local employment initiatives. The first involves Expandability, a non-profit in nearby San Jose that is trying to build a staffing company focused on workers with disabilities. The second involves Positive Resource Center, a San Francisco non-profit trying to do a pilot public service employment project, direct job creation in local government.

None of these efforts is dramatic or game-changing. But that is the way that autism employment will grow now and in the years ahead:

many local efforts, some connected to the public sector workforce, others entirely as extra-government networks, all undergirded by cultural changes inside and outside the workplace; all rooted in understanding the broader movements of the national economy.

We are not certain of the mix of initiatives to be implemented or how to achieve the cultural changes. As we have so far, we will learn, adapt, and pivot as we try various approaches. We try to eschew magical thinking about autism and know that improvements in autism employment will be gradual—even as we also know that we are in this for the long run.

Notes

1 Introduction

Among recent books that include thoughtful discussions and insights on autism and employment strategies are Scott Standifer, *Adult Autism & Employment: A Guide for Vocational Rehabilitation Professionals*, University of Missouri Press, Columbia, Missouri, 2009; Chantal Sicile-Kira and Jeremy Sicile-Kiri, *A Full Life with Autism*, Palgrave MacMillan, New York, 2012; also Gail Hawkins, *How to Find Work That Works For People with Asperger Syndrome*, Jessica Kingsley Publishers, London, 2004.

Chapter 1

2   Several books have appeared in the past few years about how we all must think of ourselves as start-ups: constantly reinventing ourselves, making contacts, learning new skills. These books have good advice in general for job seekers. We read these books, though, and think of the executive skills gaps of our members and know that a broader support system is needed in our autism community for best implementation of these strategies. See Reid Hoffman and Ben Casnocha, *The Start-up of You*, Crown Business, New York, 2012; Maynard Webb, *Rebooting Work*, Jossey-Bass, San Francisco, 2013.

Chapter 2

3   Dr. Lou joined with four other parents of autistic sons to establish the MIND Institute, stating, "As a cardiologist I witnessed daily the successes of medical science in the attack on heart diseases. With Mark's diagnosis I became consumed by a passion to bring the same power toward understanding autism's cause and finding its cure."

4   Louis Vismara, "With Housing That Caters to All, We All Win," *Sacramento Bee*, September 18, 2009.

5   Michael Tortorello, "The Architecture of Autism," *New York Times*, October 9, 2013.

6   http://bigwaveproject.org/who-we-are/about/

Chapter 3

7   For discussion of growth in autism numbers see, National Institute of Child Health And Human Development, "How Many People Are Affected by ASD?," www.nichd.nih.gov, 2014; Developmental Disabilities Institute, "Autism Facts & Statistics," www.ddiny.org, 2014; United States Centers for Disease Control and Prevention, "Autistic Spectrum Disorders," www.cdc.gov, 2014.

8   Developmental Disabilities Institute, Autism Facts & Statistics, www.ddiny.org, 2014; Autism Speaks, "How Common is Autism," www.autismspeaks.org; 2014.

9   CNN, "CDC: U.S. kids with autism up 78% in past decade," www.cnn.com, March 29, 2012.

10 Ibid.

11 Autism Speaks, "What Causes Autism?," www.autismspeaks.org; 2014.

12 National Institute of Child Health And Human Development, "What Causes Autism Spectrum Disorder," www.nichd.nih.gov, 2014

13 Autism Society, "Autism Causes," www.autism-society.org, 2014.

14 John Elder Robison's recent books exploring autism include, *Look Me in the Eye, Be Different*, and *Raising Cubby (A Father and Son's Adventures with Asperger's Trains, Tractors and High Explosives)*.

Chapter 4

15 Paul Shattuck, Sarah Carter Narendorf, "Postsecondary Education and Employment Among Youth With an Autism Spectrum Disorder," *Pediatrics*, May 14, 2012.

16 Within the first two years after high school, more than 50 percent of youth with autism had no job experience, college, or vocational education.

17 Lindsey Tanner, "New Jobs Crisis: Unemployment Autistic Adults," *Associated Press*, May 14, 2012.

18 Dawn Hendricks, "Employment and Adults with Autism Spectrum Disorders" *Journal of Vocational Rehabilitation,* 32 (2010), 125–134.

19 U.S. Bureau of Labor Statistics, "Persons with a Disability: Labor Force Characteristics Technical Note," www.bls.gov, 2013.

20 U.S. Bureau of Labor Statistics, "Persons with a Disability: Barriers to Employment, Types of Assistance, and other Labor Related Issues—May 2012," www.bls.gov, February 2012.

21 Andrew Houtenville and Mary Daly, "Employment Declines among People with Disabilities" in *The Decline in Employment of People with Disabilities: A Policy Puzzle*, David Stapleton and Richard Burkhasuer, eds. W.E. Upjohn Institute for Employment Research, Kalamazoo, Michigan, pp. 87–113.

22 Autism Speaks, "Adult Employment: New Allies Come on Board," www.autismspeaks.org; February 2014.

23 David Autor, "The Unsustainable Rise in the Disability Rolls in the United States: Causes, Consequences, and Policy Options," National Bureau of Economic Research, Washington DC, December 2011.

24 David Autor and Mark Duggan, "Supporting Work: A Proposal for Modernizing the U.S. Disability Insurance System," Center for American Progress/The Hamilton Project, Washington D.C., 2010.

25 Mary Daly, "Reforming Social Security Disability Insurance: Lessons from European Nations," Statement to the House Committee on Ways and Means Subcommittee on Social Security, June 19, 2013.

26 California Department of Employment, "Eleventh Annual NEPH Week to Emphasize Utilization of Labor," Newsletter, October 1955.

27 California Department of Employment, "Physically Handicapped Placement Figures Reflect Increasing Employer Acceptance," Newsletter, 1957.

Chapter 5

28 Stanley Greenspan and Serena Wieder, *Engaging Autism: The Floortime Approach to Helping Children Relate, Communicate and Think*, Perseus Books, New York, 2003.

29 Oliver Sacks, *An Anthropologist on Mars*, Random House, New York, 1995.

30 Thomas Sowell, "Don't Let Them Put Labels on Your Children," *San Francisco Examiner*, May 21, 1993.

31 Thomas Sowell, *Late Talking Children*, Basic Books, New York, 1997.

Chapter 6

32 Richard Vedder, Jonathan Robe, and Christopher Denhart, "Why Are Recent College Graduates Underemployed? University Enrollments and Labor Market Realities," Center for College Affordability and Productivity, Washington DC, January 2013; Allie Bidwell, "Millions of Graduates Hold Jobs that Don't Require a College Degree," *The Chronicle of Higher Education,* January 28, 2013; Jaison Abel, Richard Deitz, Yaquin Su, "Are Recent College Graduates Finding Good Jobs?," *Current Issues,* Federal Reserve Bank of New York, Volume 20, No. 1, 2014; also, Catherine Rampell, "It Takes a B.A. to Find a Job as File Clerk," *New York Times*, February 19, 2013.

Chapter 7

33 Scott Winship, "A Decade of Slack Labor Markets," www.brookings.edu blog, September 9, 2011.

34 Steven Greenhouse, "A Part-Time Life, as Hours Shrink and Shift," *New York Times*, October 27, 2012

35 Tina Brown, "The Gig Economy," *The Daily Beast*, www.thedaily-beast.com, January 27, 2009.

36 At the center is globalization. Though few recognized in the 1950s and 1960s, the post-World War II economic dominance of the United States was a brief interlude, built in good part on the devastation of the European and Asian economies in World War II. By the 1970s, Europe and Asia had rebuilt their economies, and begun to catch up with the United States. By the early 1980s, American-based manufacturing firms found themselves in global competition; and in the next decade, this competition extended to firms in finance, business services, accounting, information technology, and even education.

37 Henry Farber, "Employment Insecurity: The Decline in Worker-Firm Attachment in the United States," Princeton University Center for Economic Policy Studies, Princeton, New Jersey, 2008. Additional discussion by Professor Farber of the decline in job security is contained in "Job Loss and the Decline in Job Security in the United States" in Katherine Abraham, James Spletzer, Michael Harper, editors, *Labor in the New Economy*, University of Chicago Press, Chicago, Illinois, 2010.

38 As might be expected, job tenure results for men and women in the public sector showed an increase in average tenure for men and women during the 1973–2006 period, leading Professor Farber to note that "the public sector has been less susceptible to the competitive forces . . . causing the changes in the private sector."

Chapter 8

39 When I (Michael Bernick) went to the state of California employment office near Melrose Avenue in Los Angeles in May 1970 to look for a summer job, the job openings were all listed on 3x5 cards on wall boards. I found a job listing that was near my

neighborhood, a small collection agency in Hollywood that was seeking office assistance. I took down the information and called the employer. I went to the employer's office that day and started work the next day. You could do that in 1970.

40 In 1995, Monster.com reported 7,000 job openings per day and around 15,000 daily visitors to the site. By 1998, 50,000 job openings were being posted each day on the Monster website, with daily visitors climbing to over 650,000. By 2001 CareerBulder. com had an average of 300,000 jobs at any time, and over 25,000 employers represented.

41 Monster.com, for example, added MonsterTrak, targeting college students and Monstermoving, providing relocation services.

42 Mark Emery Bolles and Richard Nelson Bolles, *Guide to Job-Hunting Online*, Ten Speed Press, Berkeley, California, 2012 (6th edition).

43 Bolles also argues that the supersites' national and international range has little value to the job seeker looking in a particular city or region because the millions of visitors on these board and ease of résumé submission means that employers often are overwhelmed and ignore all submissions.

44 Many Bay Area residents know "Uncle Marty" from his career advice on the radio. On KGO, Marty featured the three-minute "career makeover." Marty would walk callers through redoing their résumés or recognizing their transferable skills or improving their interviewing techniques. If they felt stuck in a job, he would guide them in ways of improving their skills or seeking out a new employer or field.

45 Marty Nemko, "Finding a Job: What if Networking Doesn't Work?," www.martynemko.com, 2013.

46 Marty Nemko, "A Shortcut to Your Dream Job," www.martynemko. com, 2013.

47 Nelson Schwartz, "In Hiring, a Friend in Need is a Prospect, Indeed," *New York Times*, January 27, 2013.

48 *Ibid.* The consultant, Mr. John Sullivan, added this about Monster and the other supersites: that applicants from supersites are "Homers," after Homer Simpson.

49 Panos Ipeirotis, "Crowdsourcing and the End of Job Interviews," www.behind-the-enemy-lines.com, February 23, 2012.

50 Richard Bolles, *What Color is Your Parachute?*, initially self-published in December 1970, and subsequently published by Ten Speed Press, Berkeley, California, 1972.

Chapter 9

51 Dan Asher, *Cracking the Hidden Job Market: How to Find Opportunity in any Economy,* Ten Speed Press, Berkeley, California, 2010.

52 Duncan Mathison and Martha Finney, *Unlock the Hidden Job Market: 6 Steps to a Successful Job Search When Times are Tough*, FT Press, Upper Saddle River, New Jersey, 2009.

53 Susan Adams, "Getting a Job Using the Hidden Job Market," *Forbes*, July 5, 2011.

54 Reid Hoffman and Ben Casnocha, *The Start-up of You: Adapt to the Future, Invest in Yourself, and Transform Your Career,* Crown Business, New York, 2012.

55 Marty Nemko, "Networking is Overrated," www.martynemko.com, Sept. 16, 2012.

Chapter 10

56 Norman Maclean, *A River Runs Through It*, University of Chicago Press, Chicago, Illinois, 1976.

Chapter 11

57 Gareth Cook, "The Autism Advantage," *New York Times*, November 29, 2012.

58 "Governor Markell Welcomes the Specialisterne Foundation to Delaware," *News of Delaware*, www.news.deleware.gov, June 15, 2012.

59 Email from Thorkil Sonne to ARC of San Francisco, December 24, 2013.

60 "Company Built Around Seeing 'Heightened Ability' Where Others See Disability Lands Inaugural Clients," PRWeb, www.preweb.com, November 12, 2013.

61 Ibid.

62 Shirley Wang, "How Autism Can Help You Land a Job," *Wall Street Journal*, March 27, 2014.

63 "Software company hires autistic adults for specialized skills," CBS News—Boston, www.cbsnews.com, June 10, 2014.

64 Joshua Kendall, "New, better workers on the autism spectrum," CNN Money, www.management.fortune.cnn.com, July 23, 2013.

65 Shirley Wang, Op Cit.; also Derek Loosvelt, "Are Employees with Autism Better Employees?," Vault Career Intelligence, www.vault.com, March 28, 2014.

66 "Israeli Army Signs Up 'Rain Man' Image Analysts," ANSAmed, February 20, 2014; Joshua Kendall, Op Cit.

Chapter 12

67 Michael Mandel, "San Francisco and the Tech/Info Boom," South Mountain Economics LLC, April 2014. In the same three-year period, the City gained a total of 67,000 jobs, with the tech boom showing spin-off employment gains in other industries of construction, hospitality and finance.

69 Tomio Geron, "Airbnb and the Unstoppable Rise of the Share Economy," *Forbes*, February 11, 2013.

70 David L. Birch, *Job Creation in America: How Our Smallest Companies Put the Most People to Work*, Free Press, New York, 1987.

Chapter 13

71 Walter Powell and Kaisa Snellman, "The Knowledge Economy," *Annual Review of Sociology*, vol. 30, 2004, 1999–220.

72 Enrico Moretti, *The New Geography of Jobs*, Houghton Mifflin Harcourt, New York 2012.

73 Lawrence Katz and Claudia Goldin, *The Race Between Education and Technology*, Harvard University Press, Cambridge, Mass. 2008.

Chapter 14

74 Scott Standifer, "Reinventing Roses for Autism," *Disability Policy & Studies, University of Missouri*, December 2011.

75 Susan Ladika, "Companies Find Fruitful Results when Hiring Autistic Workers," www.workforce.com, July 16, 2012.

76 Ms. Heather Davis, the prime mover behind the TIAA-CREF apple orchards project had a twelve-year-old son with autism in 2012. Of her son, Davis explained that he had "enormous power of concentration and fine motor skills" which she saw as skills useful in apple orchard work—"I just saw a lot of little puzzle pieces coming together," she told an interviewer in 2012.

77 Michael Bernick, "New Ventures for Antipoverty Agencies," *Harvard Business Review*, November–December 1984.

78 In 2014, Ms. Javits is embarked on a mission to expand the REDF approach to a broader corporate initiative of contracting and employment—providing a more sustainable market for the goods and services of these enterprises, and abetting the hiring of workers from the social enterprises into these firms.

79 Scott Sandifer, "Lessons from Anderson: Walgreens' Autism Employment Initiative," *Disability Policy & Studies*, University of Missouri, July 2011.

80 James Kaletta, Douglas Binks, Richard Robinson, "Creating an Inclusive Workplace: Integrating Employees with Disabilities Into a Distribution Center Environment," *Professional Safety*, June 2012.

81 Randy Lewis, "Agent of Change: Making the Business Case for Inclusion," *Professional Safety*, June 2012.

82 Brenda Deskin, "Employing People on the Autism Spectrum: Find Out Who's Leading by Example," *Sage Achieve Ideas*, August 7, 2012.

Chapter 15

83 Barbara Ehrenreich, *Nickel and Dimed: On (Not) Getting By in America*, Henry Holt and Co., New York, 2001.

84 Ben Cheever, *Selling Ben Cheever: Back to Square One in a Service Economy; A Personal Odyssey*, Bloomsbury, New York, 2001.

85 Charles Platt, "Life at Wal-Mart," *Boing Boing*, February 1, 2009.

86 Adam Shepard, *Scratch Beginnings: Me, $25, and the Search for the American Dream*, HarperCollins, New York, 2008.

87 Studs Terkel, *Working: People Talk About What They Do All Day and How they Feel About What They Do*, Pantheon, New York, 1972.

88 Robert Schrank, *Ten Thousand Working Days* (MIT Press, Cambridge, Mass., 1978.). Schrank, a former Ford Foundation official, details the many jobs he has held over the fifty years of his work life. He starts in the 1920s in a furniture factory and over the next years works with his hands as a plumber, coal miner, and machinist. He then turns to a career as a union official, city commissioner, and foundation official. In these latter jobs, he continues to be plagued by the thought that he is not "productive." He adds, "I must confess that since I left the shop floor I have never been able to answer that question satisfactorily for myself or my fellow union officials, or for professionals, academics, or consultants."

89 Dan Snyder, *The Cliff Walk: A Job Lost and a Life Found*, Little, Brown and Co., Boston, 1997.

90 Susan Ladika, "Companies Find Fruitful Results When Hiring Autistic Workers," www.workforce.com, July 16, 2012. Ms. Ami Klin of the Marcus Autism Center at Emory University tells the writer, Ms. Ladika, that her research shows adults with autism pay close attention to detail and following rules, to a greater extent than other workers, and are more reliable than other workers.

Chapter 16

91 John Jones, "What do OES data have to say about increasing wage inequality?," *Monthly Labor Review*, June 2009.

92 Adam Davidson, "Skills Don't Pay the Bills," *New York Times*, November 20, 2012.

93 *Ibid*. Mr. Davidson writes, "Advanced manufacturing is really complicated. Running these machines requires a basic understanding of metallurgy, physics, chemistry, pneumatics, electrical wiring and computer code. It also requires a worker with the ability to figure out what's going on when the machine isn't working properly."

94 Boston Consulting Group, "Skills Gap in U.S. Manufacturing is Less Pervasive Than Many Believe," October 15, 2012, www.bcg.com.

95 U.S. Bureau of Labor Statistics, Occupational Employment Statistics, www.bls.gov/oes.

96 *Ibid*.

97 Michael Dardia, Elisa Barbour, "Moving Up? Earnings Mobility in California," *California Policy Review*, 1(4), 2002.

98 Daniel McMurrer and Isabel Sawhill, "How Much do Americans Move Up and Down the Economic Ladder?," Washington DC, Urban Institute, 1996.

99 The minimum wage increases have been the focus of recent government activity, though economists dispute impacts on job creation and full-time work. For a summary of the dispute, see Robert Samuelson, "Minimum Wage Mirage?" *Washington Post*, January 16, 2014.

100 Stephen Kotkin, "Minding the Inequality Gap," *New York Times*, October 4, 2008.

Chapter 17

101 Laura Shumaker, *A Regular Guy: Growing Up with Autism*, Landscape Press, Lafayette, California, 2008.

102 "What is Camphill," www.camphill.org.

103 Laura Shumaker, "Autism: Everyone Has Their Own Timetable," *San Francisco Chronicle*, August 26, 2014.

104 This ARC approach as employer of record is increasingly being tested by other employment non-profits for adults with disabilities in the Bay Area. The approach has the value of providing a try-out period for employers, who are not required to go through the hiring processes or the even more disagreeable firing processes. Expandability, a nonprofit employment agency for workers with disabilities in San Jose is one of the most advanced with a staffing agency for workers with disabilities, headed by a woman with many years of experience with private sector staffing firms.

105 The sheltered workshop is sometimes referred to as a "community workshop," based on its roots in separate communities in the nineteenth century and first half of the twentieth century established for adults with disabilities. These communities, usually linked with asylums, were center on the idea of work as providing therapeutic value for clients.

106 Corey Azevedo, "Sheltered Workshops as Cooperatives," email to author, July 16, 2014.

107 New York Makes Work Pay, "Transformation of Center-based Work into Integrated Opportunities for People with Disabilities in New York: Analysis and Recommendations for Center-Based Employers," www.NYMakesWorkPay.org, 2010.

Chapter 18

108 For the evolution of federal job training programs, from MDTA, through the Comprehensive Employment and Training Act (CETA), the Job Training Partnership Act (JTPA) and the current Workforce Investment Act (WIA), see United States Department of Labor, "What is Working (and What's Not): A Summary of Research on the Economic Impacts of Employment and Training Programs," Washington DC, US Department of Labor, 1995; Gary Burtless, "Manpower Policies for the Disadvantaged: What Works?" *Brookings Review*, Fall 1984.

109 United States Department of Labor, "Congressional Budget Justification, Employment and Training Administration: FY 2014," www.dol.gov, May 2013.

110 For analysis of the public workforce training, H. Holzer and D. Nightingale, editors, *Reshaping the American Workforce in a Changing Economy*, Urban Institute Press, Washington DC, 2007, also H. Holzer, "Workforce Development As An Antipoverty Strategy: What Do We Know? What Should We Do?," *Focus*, 26, no. 2, Fall 2009, 62–68.

111 U.S. DOL, "Building American Skills Through Community Colleges," Washington DC, 2013. The community colleges are targeted for $2 billion for job training in the Health Care and Education Reconciliation Act and $500 annually in the Trade Adjustment Assistance Community College Career Training Grant Fund.

112 California Little Hoover Commission, "Serving Students, Serving California: Updating the California community Colleges to Meet Evolving Demands," Sacramento, California, February 2012.

113 *Ibid.*, also Community College League of California, "A Report on the Commission of the Future," Sacramento, California, 2011; California Community Colleges Student Success Task Force, "Advancing Student Success in California Community Colleges," Sacramento, California, 2012; California Community Colleges, "System Strategic Plan," Sacramento, California, 2013. Among the task force findings is the limited English and math skills of the majority of incoming students. Around 75 percent of entering students in the California Community Colleges are not prepared for college-level English, and 90 percent are not prepared for college level math. Further, only 54 percent of degree-seeking students in California Community Colleges ever achieve a certificate, degree, or transfer, and only 41 percent of students with goal of transferring to a four year institution ever do so.

114 Already, students over thirty-five years of age are a significant percentage of the community college enrollment. In 2012, slightly more than half of the students are of the traditional college-going age, eighteen to twenty-four, with another 20 percent between the ages of twenty-five to thirty-four. Around a quarter of the student population is thirty-five years or older.

115 Thomas Edsall, "Are the Good Jobs Gone?," *New York Times*, April 17, 2013.

116 The Internet training has a number of clear advantages over classroom training for retraining. The worker can continue in a job or position and undertake the training on her own time. Or she can fit in training while working part-time. Training can be started at any time, and proceed at the worker's own pace, without waiting for specific start and end dates.

Chapter 19

117 The experiences of ASTEP and Ms. Scheiner in seeking to influence workplace culture are described more fully in Pamela Babcock, "Organization Offers Exposure to People with Asperger's Syndrome," *Society for Human Resource Management*, November 15, 2011, www.shrm.org; "Is It Time for Asperger's in the Workplace?," *Diversity Journal*, November/December 2012; Marcia Scheiner, "Improving Employment Outcomes for Individuals with Autism," *Autism Spectrum News*, Spring 2014, www.mhnews-autism.org;

118 Autism Speaks, the largest of the national advocacy groups, brought together employers and advocates in an Autism Speaks Employment Think Tank in 2012 with goals of showcasing the skills of adults with autism and increasing both employer outreach and workplace culture; Autism Speaks, "Employment Think Tank," www.autismspeaks.org, 2012.

Chapter 20

119 In the early days of the Club, a contingent of three people came from Modesto, and another contingent of three took the train in from Sacramento. They subsequently formed their own groups, in a loose confederation with us.

120 California's prominent job coach, Marty Nemko, returned to the Club recently. This time, he came not as a speaker but as part of a musical performance with a woman on the autistic spectrum, Ms. Jeffrie Givens. Nemko played the keyboard accompanying Ms. Givens on vocals. Ms. Givens had come to Nemko seeking help in her job search, after losing the $8 an hour job she had held at a music store for eight years. He learned of her avocation as a singer, and they developed a performance under the title, "Givens & Nemko in a Live Musical Tribute to Autism!" In introducing the performance, Nemko wrote, "As a young child, they called Jeffrie Givens retarded. Then they called her shy, very shy. Then she was diagnosed with Asperger's. Now they call her amazing. She has a solid day job as a researcher and an even better night job as a singer and actor. In the last five years, she has performed for thousands of people." Working with Nemko as job coach, Ms. Givens did get a job as a researcher at Children's Hospital in Oakland, where she continues to be employed today.

121 As early as the 1830s, Alexis de Tocqueville could celebrate the strength of voluntary associations in his journeys through America, and his observations ring true today. Alexis de Tocqueville, *Democracy in America*, Penguin Classics, New York, 2003.

122 WrongPlanet.net, a lively online network of adults with autism, advocates and family members; AutisticsSpeak.wordpress.com.

123 Walter Shapiro, "CETA: A '70s Government Jobs Program That Didn't Work," www.politicsdaily.com, November 19, 2009. Among the research on CETA public service employment, I include material on CETA public service employment in my

book on San Francisco's job employment programs, *The Dreams of Jobs* (1984), and other studies can be found in Richard Nathan, *Monitoring the Public Service Employment Program*, Brookings Institute, Washington DC, 1979, Robert Cook, Charles Adams, V. Lane Hawkins, "The Public Service Employment Program," Upjohn Institute, Kalamazoo, Michigan, 1985.

124 In 2009, Noah's brother Karl, published a memoir of growing up with Noah, and Noah's years during and after Fairview. Karl Taro Greenfeld, *Boy Alone: A Brother's Memoir*, Harper Collins, New York, 2009.

Acknowledgements

Our editor, Niels Aaboe, developed and shaped this book from its origin as an essay that first appeared in *Zocalo Public Square*. He believes that a better system of employment for adults with autism can be built. We agree, and are grateful for his commitment and guidance.

Most of the persons who contributed to this book are included in the pages above. Additionally, we would like to acknowledge a number of others in our autism community for their contributions: Bruno Peguese, Jane Blanchard, Iris Weiss, and Cindy Sawchuck of San Francisco; Katie Brown, Brian Johnson, and Bryan Fauth of California State University East Bay; and Paul Hippolitus of UC Berkeley.

We want to acknowledge several professionals in employment for workers with autism and other neurological differences who contributed to our research: Max Forman, former director of Jobs for All; Catherine Kelly Baird, former Director of the California Governor's Committee on Employment of People with Disabilities; Catherine Campisi, former Director of the California State Department of Rehabilitation; and Gloria Castaneda and Doug Gordy of the Media Access Project.

Peter Richardson, teacher, writer and editor in Berkeley, reviewed various sections of the manuscript and provided ideas for addressing autism employment in the context of broader employment trends; as did in different ways, Kevin Hollenbeck of the Upjohn Institute; Professor Jack Pitney of Claremont McKenna College, Kris Stadelman, Executive Director of the NOVA Workforce Investment Board in Silicon Valley, and NOVA job counselors Connie Brock and Camille Grabowski; Chris Thornberg of Beacon Economics; and Michael Larsen of Larsen Pomada.

We would be remiss if we did not close with the contribution of Mayra Montalvo, who served as line editor and word processing expert. The content and opinions in this book are those of the authors and do not represent those of the Bureau of Labor Statistics, the U.S. Department of Labor, or the federal government.

About the Authors

Michael Bernick served as director of the California labor department, the California Employment Development Department, from 1999 through 2004. Since 2004, he has been a Research Fellow with the Milken Institute and Counsel to the Sedgwick law firm, headquartered in San Francisco. He has been involved in job training on the local and state levels for over thirty-four years. He is a graduate of Harvard College, Oxford University (Balliol College), and the University of California, Berkeley, School of Law.

Richard Holden has been analyzing labor markets, regional economies and the nexus between economies and public policy for thirty years, ranging from U.S. border employment studies to California earthquake risk and labor markets. He has been the regional commissioner for the U.S. Bureau of Labor Statistics in San Francisco since 2004. Prior to this he served as research director of the California Employment Development Department, leading a staff of 300 research analysts, technical staff, and economists. Holden has a B.A. in economics from the University of New Mexico and a masters in Public Affairs from the University of Texas, Austin.

Index